Python Acer

- A Python Developer's Guide

TO CRACK PYTHON INTERVIEW

V. Hanuman Kumar, Ph.D

NOTION PRESS

NOTION PRESS

India. Singapore. Malaysia.

ISBN xxx-x-xxxxx-xx-x

Dedicated to Dearest

"Anuhya" & Dhatrika

Table Of Contents

Foreword

V. Hanuman Kumar, is a certified data science & machine learning professional and have strong research expertise in computer science engineering. Dr. Hanuman authored research articles on machine learning, data science, computerized bionics and python programming. He worked with various machine learning algorithms with the advent of data science concepts to solve business problems. In authors works the major area of concern is data science with python programming language.

The word "data science" has appeared in various contexts over the past thirty years but did not become an established term until recently. The trendy definition of "data science" sketched during the second Japanese-French statistics symposium organized at the University of Montpellier II (France) in 1992.

Every day in world, that is increasingly becoming a digital space, organizations deal with zettabytes and yottabytes of structured and unstructured data. Evolving technologies like data science & analytics, machine learning have enabled cost savings and smarter storage spaces to store and process data critical data.

Currently, in the industry, there is a huge demand for skillful and certified data scientists, data analysts and python developers. They are among the highest-paid professionals in the information technology industry. According to Forbes, 'the best job in America is of a data scientist with an average annual salary of $110,000'. Only a few people have the potential to process and derive valuable insights out of data. The author's work in this book will definitely create a road map for the data science and machine-learning aspirants to get success in their future endeavors with a great potential.

Mr. Prasad
Sr. Business Analyst
Shell India Markets Pvt. Ltd., Bangalore
10-10-2023

Preface

The book titled **"Python Acer – A Python Developer's Guide",** To crack python interview gives a pathway to clear python interviews to start career in python world, might routes to data science, machine learning and data analytics as well. To solve business problems, this book presents the necessary skills with some examples by replicating the industry needs developed in python programming language. The examples presented in this book, implemented by using PyCharm IDE with Python3.

Dr. V. Hanuman Kumar, Ph. D

10-10-2023

Acknowledgments

It is my privilege to convey my sincere acknowledges to **Mr. Poornachandra Rao & Associates, Charted Accountants, Chirala** for his support during the initiation of services from Data Qzen Software Solutions and Research Pvt. Ltd.

It is my privilege to convey my happy wishes to **Mr. Ramanakanth Mannem** for his support during the journey to make this book happen.

I am very much desire to convey my gratitude and affection to my parents, sister and brother

Mr. Vudata Leela Krishna Babu

Mrs. Padmavati and

Mrs. T Mahalakshmi

Mr. V. Ramprasad

About The Book

"Python Acer – A Python Developer's Guide", is your comprehensive guide to preparing for and succeeding in Python job interviews. Whether you're aiming for a Python developer, data scientist, or web developer role, this book equips you with the knowledge, skills, and confidence you need to stand out in the competitive job market. With a thorough understanding of Python fundamentals, best practices, and interview strategies, you'll be well-prepared to secure your dream job and advance your career in Python development.

In today's tech-driven world, Python has become one of the most sought-after programming languages. Whether you're a seasoned Python developer or a newcomer looking to break into the field, landing your dream Python job often hinges on your ability to perform well in interviews.

"Python Acer – A Python Developer's Guide" is your indispensable guide to preparing for and acing Python job interviews.

Understanding the Python Landscape

- Explore the importance of Python in the tech industry
- Discover the various job roles and industries where Python is in high demand
- Gain insights into the latest trends and developments in the Python ecosystem

Crafting the Perfect Resume

- Learn how to tailor your resume to make it stand out to potential employers
- Highlight your Python skills and experience effectively
- Understand the importance of showcasing your projects and contributions

Nailing the Technical Screening

- Master the art of coding challenges and technical assessments
- Solve common Python coding problems with detailed explanations
- Explore best practices for tackling algorithmic and data structure questions

Python Fundamentals

- Brush up on essential Python concepts, including data types, variables, and operators
- Dive into control structures, loops, and conditional statements
- Explore functions, modules, and libraries that are commonly used in Python development

Object-Oriented Programming (OOP)

- Deepen your understanding of OOP principles in Python
- Learn how to create and work with classes and objects

- Explore inheritance, encapsulation, and polymorphism

Python Libraries and Frameworks

- Familiarize yourself with popular Python libraries and frameworks
- Learn about web frameworks like Flask for web development interviews

Database Integration

- Understand the basics of database systems and SQL
- Learn how to interact with databases using Python

Web Development with Python

- Dive into web development concepts, including HTTP, RESTful APIs, and HTTP methods
- Showcase your ability to design and develop web applications

Python Best Practices

- Discuss code quality, maintainability, and readability
- Explore testing and debugging strategies

Behavioral and Soft Skills

- Prepare for behavioral interview questions
- Enhance your communication and problem-solving skills
- Learn how to demonstrate teamwork and adaptability

Mock Interviews and Practice Questions

- Access a collection of Python interview questions and solutions
- Engage in mock interviews to build confidence and refine your interview skills
- Receive guidance on handling technical interviews effectively

The Interview Day

- Get practical tips for the interview day, including what to wear and bring
- Learn how to manage stress and stay composed during interviews
- Understand post-interview etiquette and follow-up strategies

1. Introduction

Python is a high level general purpose language and was introduced by Guido Van Rossum. Python is commonly used for developing websites and software, task automation, data analysis and visualization.

The main **features of Python** are

- Easy to learn
- Easy to use
- Broad library
- Dynamic Typed Language
- Supports Object Oriented Programming
- Interactive
- Portable
- Extendable
- Scalable
- Versatile Database APIs

The **applications of Python** not only limited to

- Web development
- Scientific applications
- Software development
- Business applications
- Artificial Intelligence and Machine Learning

2. Mathematical Foundation

2.1. Number System: is the basic building block to implement python program and is referred with type of data.

Integers*	: {.......-3, -2, -1, 0, 1, 2, 3, etc.}	==>int*
Decimal*	: 12.3, 54.32, -34.432, etc.	==>float*
Rational	: 2/3, 3/5 --> 0.6, -2/7	
Irrational	: π, $\sqrt{3}$, $\sqrt{5}$	
Real	: Rational + Irrational	
Imaginary*	: 3i+4j	==> complex*

2.2. Arithmetic Operations:

Basic Operations: Addition, Subtraction, Multiplication, and Division

Subtraction   :   2 - 3 = -1

Multiplication :   2 X 3 = 6

Division   :   21 / 4 = quotient 5,remainder 1

BODMAS Principle- used to compute the order of precedence to evaluate an expression

Brackets	: ()
Of	: power of
	: percent of
	: fraction of
Division	: %
Multiplication	: *
Addition	: +
Subtraction	: -

Comparison :

Symbol	Words	Example Use
=	equals	1 + 1 = 2 ==> True
≠	not equal to	1 + 1 ≠ 1 ==> True
>	greater than	5 > 7 ==> False
<	less than	7 < 9 ==> True
≥	greater than or equal to	money ≥ 1
≤	less than or equal to	bill ≤ 3

2.3. Binary Number System: Used to represent number in a sequence of zeros and ones.

Decimal number = 137

Binary Number = 1000 1001

2.4. Logic Gates: Used to perform arithmetic and logic operations and are basic elementary units of computer's arithmetic and logic unit.

1 represents True

0 represents False

AND gate :

----

1 and 1 => 1	True and True* => True
1 and 0 => 0	True and False* => False
0 and 1 => 0	False* and True => False
0 and 0 => 0	False* and False => False

OR gate :

----

1 or 1 => 1	True* or True => True
1 or 0 => 1	True* or False => True
0 or 1 => 1	False or True* => True
0 or 0 => 0	False or False* => False

NOT gate:

----

not 1 => 0	not True => False
not 0 => 1	not False => True

1s compliment	==> 1101110 ==> 0010001
2s compliment	==> 1s + 1 => 0010001

2.5. SETs: Unordered collections of elements and not encourage duplicates

s1 = {1, 2, 3, 7}

s2 = {3, 4, 5, 7}

Set Union   : s1 ∪ s2 => {1,2,3,4,5,7}

Set Intersection   : s1 ∩ s2 => {3,7}

Set Difference   : s1 - s2 => {1,2}

                             : s2 - s1 => {4,5}

2.6. Sequence & Series:

Sequence:

Infinite Sequence   : 1,2,3,4,5........n   # n(n+1)/2

Finite Sequence   : 1,2,3,4,5,6,7,....1000

Backward Sequence   : 5,4,3,2,1

Alphabetical sequence : a, b, c, d, e, ...z

Negative sequence   : -1,-2,-3,-4,-5,....

                             : ....-5,-4,-3,-2,-1

Decimal → 10, 20, 30, 40, 50, 60....10000

Even → 2,4,6,8,10,12,14, ...

Square→1, 2, 4, 8, 16, 32, ...

Not a sequence→ 1,5,7,8,10,11, ...

Series :

$$\sum_{x=1}^{4} 5x$$

             STATE   : x=1 to 4, BEHAVIOR : 5x

=Solution==> = 5(1) + 5(2) + 5(3) + 5(4) = 5 + 10 + 15 + 20 = 50

2.7. Algebra:

Expression: An expression is a number, a variable, or a combination of numbers, variables and operation symbols.

        Ex: 4.5 + 1 <==> 5.5

Equation   : Equation is made up of two expressions connected by an equal sign.

        Ex: 16 - 6 = 10

           x + 8 = 40

           3*x + 4 = 5x + 14

Numeric expression: It will contain all numbers. To apply operations to numbers we can use this

Ex: 2(3 + 8)

= 6 + 8

= 14

Algebraic expression: At least one variable and at least one operation

Ex: 2(x + 8y)

Use case:

Simplify the algebraic expression: 3(4x+5y)-2(3x-7y)

Then evaluate the simplified expression for x = 3 and y = -2.

==> I. Substitute the values, get final output

Then evaluate the simplified expression for x = 2/7 and y = 3/4.

==> II. Simplify the expression, then substitute the values

Solution:

Step 1: Simplify the algebraic expression using the basic properties of real numbers.

= 3(4x+5y) - 2(3x-7y)

= 3(4x+5y) + (-2)(3x+[-7]y)   <== Definition of Subtraction

= 12x + 15y + (-6)x + 14y   <== Distributive property

= 12x + (-6)x + 15y + 14y   <== Commutative property of Addition

= (12+[-6])x + (15 + 14)y   <== Distributive property

= 6x + 29y   <== Simplify

Step 2: Now substitute x with 3 and y with -2

= 6(3) + 29(-2)

= -40

2.8.   Function : used to represent the behavior of an entity or object

Given function: f(x) = 2x + 1. Find f(x) when x = 10

Math: Equation   Question   Input data

Python: Behavior   REQ/Ticket   State

x = 10   # STATE

2x+1   # BEHAVIOR

2.9. Plane Geometry:

POLYGON (# Generalization)

TRIANGLE   QUADRILATERAL   PENTAGON   HEXAGON

- Equilateral   - Parallelogram

 - Isosceles   - Square

 - Scalene   - Rectangle

            - Rhombus

            - Trapezium

2.10.   Matrices: majorly used to represent multi dimensional data.

A[1][1][2][2]

Above is 3X3 matrix : Means 3 rows 3 columns   A[3X3]

A[2][1] ==> 2nd row,1st column ==> 32

A[1][3] ==> 1st row,3rd column ==> 5

A[2][2] ==> 2nd row,2nd column ==> 12

3. Variables

3.1. Variable:

Variable is a name that is used to refer to memory location. Python variable is also known as an identifier and used to hold value. Variable names can be a group of both the letters and digits, but they have to begin with a letter or an underscore.

3.2. Types:

There are two types of variables in Python - Local variable and Global variable.

- Local variables are the variables that declared inside the function and have scope within the function.
- Global variables can be used throughout the program, and its scope is in the entire program. We can use global variables inside or outside the function.

A variable declared outside the function is the global variable by default. Python provides the **global** keyword to use global variable inside the function. If we don't use the **global** keyword, the function treats it as a local variable.

3.3. Garbage Collection:

- The process of automatic deletion of unwanted or unused objects to free the memory
- The garbage collector in Python starts running as soon as the program's execution starts. Whenever the object's reference counter reaches 0, the garbage collector is triggered.

3.4. Assign single value to multiple variables:

A = B = C = 10

3.5. Multiple variables with multiple values:

A, B, C = 10, 'python', 16.21

→A= 10,

→ B = 'python',

→C = 16.21

3.6. Tokens: The smallest individual unit of a program.

Keywords- Keywords are the pre-defined set of words in a language that perform their specific function. You cannot assign a new value or task to them other than the pre-defined one. Ex: if, elif, while, True, False, None, break etc

Identifiers- Identifiers are the names that you can assign a value to

Literals - Literals are the fixed or constant values. They can either be string, numeric or Boolean.

Punctuators or Separators - Punctuators, also known as separators give a structure to code. They are [mostly] used to define blocks in a program. We will be covering code blocks in control flow statements ,

Single quotes – ' ' , double quote – " " , parenthesis – ( ), brackets – [ ], Braces – { },

colon – (:) , comma (,), etc.

3.7. Operators-Operators are the symbols which are used to perform operations between operands.

List of Operators:

- Arithmetic operators (+, -, /, * etc)
- Assignment operators (=)
- Comparison operators (>, <, >=, <=, ==, !=)
- Logical operators (and, or, not)
- Identity operators (is, is not)
- Membership operators (in, not in)
- Bitwise operators (&, |, ^ etc)

Types of Operators:

- **Unary Operators**: Operators having single operand.

  Ex: +8, -7, etc

- **Binary Operators:** Operators working on 2 operands.

  Ex: 2+2, 4-3, 8*9, etc.

- **Ternary Operators:** work on 3 operands and so on.

  These are just basics and not so important to know but the operators listed below are very important

4. **IDE PyCharm:**

PyCharm is a popular integrated development environment (IDE) specifically designed for Python programming. It is developed by Jet Brains, a company known for creating powerful and user-friendly developer tools. PyCharm provides a wide range of features and tools to streamline the Python development process and enhance your coding experience. Here are some key features and aspects of PyCharm:

1. **Code Editor and Intelligent Code Completion**: PyCharm offers a feature-rich code editor with syntax highlighting, auto-indentation, and intelligent code completion. It suggests code completions, function names, and variable names as you type, which can significantly speed up coding and reduce errors.

   Code Navigation and Refactoring: PyCharm makes it easy to navigate through your codebase. You can quickly jump to definitions, find usages of variables or functions, and refactor code to improve its structure and readability.

2. **Debugging Tools**: The built-in debugger in PyCharm allows you to set breakpoints, step through code, inspect variables, and identify and fix issues in your code. It provides a visual interface for debugging, making the process more intuitive.

3. **Version Control Integration**: PyCharm seamlessly integrates with version control systems like Git, allowing you to manage and track changes to your code. You can commit, pull, push, and resolve merge conflicts directly from the IDE.

4. **Project Management**: PyCharm helps you manage your projects effectively. You can create, open, and organize projects, and it provides tools for managing project dependencies and virtual environments.

5. **Integrated Terminal**: PyCharm includes an integrated terminal that allows you to execute shell commands and scripts without leaving the IDE. This is particularly useful for running tests, managing packages, and performing various development tasks.

6. **Python Console and Scientific Tools**: PyCharm provides an interactive Python console that allows you to experiment with code snippets and test ideas. It also offers integration with popular scientific libraries like NumPy, SciPy, and Matplotlib.

7. **Web Development Support**: PyCharm offers support for web development using frameworks like Django and Flask. It provides features for template editing, project configuration, and debugging web applications.

8. **Code Analysis and Inspections**: PyCharm performs static code analysis and offers code inspections to identify potential issues, such as syntax errors, unused variables, or code smells. This helps you write cleaner and more maintainable code.

9. **Extensibility**: PyCharm supports plugins and extensions, allowing you to customize the IDE according to your needs. You can install plugins for additional features, themes, and integrations.

PyCharm comes in two editions: the Community edition (free and open-source) and the Professional edition (paid, with additional advanced features). The choice between the two depends on your requirements and the complexity of your projects.

Overall, PyCharm is a powerful and versatile IDE that can significantly boost your productivity and help you develop high-quality Python applications efficiently.

Installing PyCharm on Windows:

1. **Download PyCharm**:

   - Visit the official PyCharm website: https://www.jetbrains.com/pycharm/

   - Click on the "Download" button for the version you want (Community or Professional).

2. **Run the Installer**:

- Locate the downloaded installer file (**.exe**) and double-click on it.

- Follow the on-screen instructions to install PyCharm.

- You can choose the installation location and customize settings during the installation process.

3. **Launch PyCharm**:

   - Once the installation is complete, you can launch PyCharm from the Start menu or desktop shortcut.

   - PyCharm may prompt you to import settings from a previous installation or configure your preferences. You can choose to do this or skip it for now.

Installing PyCharm on macOS:

1. **Download PyCharm**:

   - Visit the official PyCharm website: https://www.jetbrains.com/pycharm/

   - Click on the "Download" button for the version you want (Community or Professional).

2. **Mount the Disk Image**:

   - Locate the downloaded **.dmg** file in your Downloads folder or the specified download location.

   - Double-click on the **.dmg** file to mount the disk image.

3. **Drag to Applications**:

   - A new window will appear showing the PyCharm application icon.

   - Simply drag the PyCharm icon and drop it onto the "Applications" folder icon to install PyCharm.

4. **Launch PyCharm**:

   - Go to your Applications folder.

- Find PyCharm and double-click on it to launch the application.

- PyCharm may prompt you to import settings from a previous installation or configure your preferences. You can choose to do this or skip it for now.

Setting Up PyCharm:

1. **Create or Open a Project**:

   - After launching PyCharm, you can create a new project or open an existing one. A project is a container for your Python code and related files.

2. **Configure Python Interpreter**:

   - PyCharm needs to know which Python interpreter to use for your projects. It's recommended to use a virtual environment for each project.

   - If you don't have a virtual environment set up, PyCharm can help you create one. You can also configure an existing interpreter.

3. **Start Coding**:

   - Once your project is set up and the interpreter is configured, you can start writing Python code in PyCharm's code editor.

Remember that PyCharm offers a free Community edition as well as a paid Professional edition with advanced features. You can choose the edition that best suits your needs.

5. Operators

Operators are special symbols in python that carry out arithmetic or logical computation. The value that the operator operates on called as operand.

5.1. Arithmetic operators used to perform mathematical operations like addition, subtraction, multiplication etc.

Operator	Semantics	Example
+	Addition	5+5→ 10
-	Subtraction	5-4→ 1
*	Multiplication	2*3→ 6
/	Division	30/3→ 10
%	Modulus	10%4→ 2
//	Quotient	18//5→ 3
**	Exponent	3**5→243

5.2. Comparison operators

Comparison operators used to compare data values. It returns either *True* or *False* according to the condition.

Operator	Semantics	Example
>	Greater than - True if left operand is greater than the right	x > y
<	Less than - True if left operand is less than the right	x < y
==	Equal to - True if both operands are equal	x == y
!=	Not equal to - True if operands are not equal	x != y
>=	Greater than or equal to - True if left operand is greater than or equal to the	x >= y

	right	
<=	Less than or equal to - True if left operand is less than or equal to the right	x <= y

5.3. Logical operators

Logical operators are and, *or, not* operators.

Operator	Semantics	Example
and	True if both the operands are true	x and y
or	True if either of the operands is true	x or y
not	True if operand is false (complements the operand)	not x

5.4. Bitwise operators

Bitwise operators act on operands as if they were string of binary digits. It operates bit by bit, hence the name.

Ex: Assume x = 10 (0000 1010 in binary) and y = 4 (0000 0100 in binary)

Operator	Semantics	Example
&	Bitwise AND	x& y = 0 (0000 0000)
|	Bitwise OR	x | y = 14 (0000 1110)
~	Bitwise NOT	~x = -11 (1111 0101)
^	Bitwise XOR	x ^ y = 14 (0000 1110)
>>	Bitwise right shift	x>> 2 = 2 (0000 0010)
<<	Bitwise left shift	x<< 2 = 40 (0010 1000)

5.5. Assignment operators

Assignment operators used to assign values to variables.

For example X = 5 is simple assignment, that assigns the value 5 on the right to the variable **X** on the left. There are various compound operators like **X += 5** that adds to the variable and later assigns the same. It is equivalent to **X = X + 5**. Some of the operators listed in below table.

Operator	Symantics	Example
=	x = 5	x = 5
+=	x = x + 5	x += 5
-=	x = x - 5	x -= 5
*=	x = x * 5	x *= 5
/=	x = x / 5	x /= 5
%=	x = x % 5	x %= 5
//=	x = x // 5	x //= 5
**=	x = x ** 5	x **= 5
&=	x = x & 5	x &= 5
|=	x = x | 5	x |= 5
^=	x = x ^ 5	x ^= 5
>>=	x = x >> 5	x >>= 5
<<=	x = x << 5	x <<= 5

5.6. Identity operators used to check, if two values (or variables) are located on the same part of the memory. Two variables that are equal does not imply that they are identical.

Operator	Semantics	Example
Is	True if the operands are identical (refer to the same object)	x is y, here is results in 1 if id(x) equals id(y).
is not	True if the operands are not identical	x is not y, here is not results in 1 if id(x) is not equal to id(y).

5.7. Membership operators

in and **not in** are the membership operators in python. They used to test whether a value or variable found in a sequence (Let X be string, list, tuple, set and dictionary).

Operator	Semantics	Example
In	True if value/variable is found in the sequence	6 in X
not in	True if value/variable is not found in the sequence	6 not in X

6 . Data Types

6.1. Numbers: INT, FLOAT, COMPLEX

- x = 10 # int
- x = 10.4 # float
- x = int(x) # Convert to int
- x = float(x) # Convert to float

6.2. Boolean: BOOL

- Boolean → True or false
- it occupies 1 bit of memory location
- True as 1
- False as 0

6.3. Data Structures:

- String →"hello "
- List→[1,2,'h',10.2]
- Tuple→(1, 2, 4, 6)
- Dictionary →{1:'hai', 2:'war'}
- Set→{12, 34, 1, 6}

6.4. CRUD – Create Read (Retrieve) Update Delete:

→CREATE

x = 10

→ RETRIEVE

print ("Value of x : ", x)

→UPDATE

x = 20

print("Value of x : ", x)

→DELETE

del x

7. Keywords

Keywords are the reserved words in Python. We cannot use a keyword as a variable name, function name or any other identifier.

>>> import keyword

>>> print (keyword. kwlist)

Keyword	Description
and	A logical operator
as	To create an alias
assert	For debugging
break	To break out of a loop
class	To define a class
continue	To continue to the next iteration of a loop
def	To define a function
del	To delete an object
elif	Used in conditional statements, same as else if
else	Used in conditional statements
except	Used with exceptions, what to do when an exception occurs
False	Boolean value, result of comparison operations
finally	Used with exceptions, a block of code that will be executed no matter if there is an exception or not
for	To create a for loop
from	To import specific parts of a module
global	To declare a global variable
if	To make a conditional statement
import	To import a module
in	To check if a value is present in a list, tuple, etc.
is	To test if two variables are equal
lambda	To create an anonymous function
None	Represents a null value
nonlocal	To declare a non-local variable

not	A logical operator
or	A logical operator
pass	A null statement, a statement that will do nothing
raise	To raise an exception
return	To exit a function and return a value
True	Boolean value, result of comparison operations
try	To make a try...except statement
while	To create a while loop
With	Used to simplify exception handling
Yield	To end a function, returns a generator

8. Decision Making

If-else statements: The **if-else** statement allows you to execute different blocks of code based on a condition. Here's an example:

```python
x = 10
if x > 0:
    print("x is positive")
else:
    print("x is non-positive")
```

Elif statements: If you have multiple conditions to check, you can use **elif** (short for "else if") statements. Here's an example:

```python
x = 10
if x > 0:
print("x is positive")
elif x == 0:
print("x is zero")
else:
print("x is negative")
```

Nested if statements: You can nest **if** statements inside other **if** statements to handle more complex conditions. Here's an example:

```python
x = 10
if x > 0:
if x < 100:
print("x is positive and less than 100")
else:
print("x is positive but greater than or equal to 100")
else:
print("x is non-positive")
```

Ternary operator: Python also provides a concise way to write simple conditional expressions using the ternary operator. Here's an example:

```python
x = 10
message = "x is positive" if x > 0 else "x is non-positive"
print(message)
```

9. Loops

Python provides two main types of loops, **for** loops and **while** loops, which allow you to iterate over sequences of data or repeatedly execute a block of code as long as a certain condition is met. Loops are essential for automating repetitive tasks and processing collections of data. Let's explore each type of loop:

9.1 for Loops:

A **for** loop is used to iterate over a sequence (such as a list, tuple, string, or range) and execute a block of code for each item in the sequence.

for item in sequence: # Code to execute for each item

For example, here's how you could use a **for** loop to print each element of a list:

fruits = ["apple", "banana", "cherry"]

for fruit in fruits:

print(fruit)

9.2 while Loops:

A **while** loop is used to repeatedly execute a block of code as long as a specified condition is **True**.

while condition:

 # Code to execute as long as condition is True

Here's an example of a **while** loop that counts from 1 to 5:

count = 1

while count <= 5:

print(count)

count += 1

10. Control Statements

Python loops also support control statements that allow you to modify the loop's behavior:

- **break**: Terminates the loop prematurely, even if the loop condition is still **True**.
- **continue**: Skips the current iteration and moves to the next iteration of the loop.
- **else** with **for** and **while** loops: This block of code is executed when the loop completes normally (i.e., when the loop condition becomes **False**).

for item in sequence:

if condition:

break # Exit the loop

if another_condition:

continue # Skip this iteration

else:

 # Code to execute if loop completes normally

Nested Loops:

You can also nest loops within each other to create more complex iterations. This is useful for working with multidimensional data or when you need to perform actions on combinations of items from different sequences.

For i in range(3):

for j in range(2):

print(i, j)

This nested loop example prints pairs of numbers from 0 to 2 and 0 to 1.

Loops are powerful constructs that allow you to automate tasks and process data efficiently. They are essential for handling repetitive operations and working with collections in Python.

11. Data Structures

Python offers a variety of built-in data structures that allow you to organize, store, and manipulate data in different ways. These data structures are fundamental tools for solving a wide range of programming problems. Here are some of the most commonly used data structures in Python:

1. **Lists**: Lists are ordered collections of items. They can hold elements of different data types, and you can modify, add, or remove items from them.

   my_list = [1, 2, 3, "hello", True]

2. **Tuples**:Tuples are similar to lists but are immutable, meaning their elements cannot be changed after creation.

   my_tuple = (1, 2, 3, "hello", True)

3. **Strings**:Strings are sequences of characters and are also considered a data structure. They are immutable, like tuples.

   my_string = "Hello, Python!"

4. **Sets**:Sets are unordered collections of unique elements. They are useful for tasks like eliminating duplicates from a sequence.

   my_set = {1, 2, 3, 3, 4, 5}

5. **Dictionaries**:Dictionaries are key-value pairs, where each value is associated with a unique key. They are useful for representing structured data.

   my_dict = {"name": "Alice", "age": 25, "city": "New York"}

6. **Lists of Lists (Nested Lists)**:You can have lists inside lists to create more complex data structures, such as matrices or multi-dimensional arrays.

   matrix = [[1, 2, 3], [4, 5, 6], [7, 8, 9]]

7. **Lists of Tuples (List of Pairs)**: Similar to nested lists, you can have lists of tuples for representing pairs of related data.

   pairs = [("apple", 3), ("banana", 2), ("cherry", 5)]

8. **Stacks and Queues (Using Lists)**: You can implement stacks (Last-In-First-Out) and queues (First-In-First-Out) using lists by manipulating their elements.

   stack = [3, 2, 1] queue = [1, 2, 3]

9. **Deque (Collections module)**:The **collections** module provides a **deque** (double-ended queue) data structure, which is optimized for fast append and pop operations from both ends.

from collections import deque

my_deque = deque([1, 2, 3])

10. **Hashable Collections (Collections module)**: The **collections** module also offers hashable collections like **defaultdict** and **Counter** for specialized use cases.

from collections import defaultdict,

Counter word_freq = Counter(["apple", "banana", "apple", "cherry"])

These data structures provide a foundation for organizing and manipulating data efficiently in Python. Choosing the right data structure for a specific problem is essential for writing clean, efficient, and maintainable code.

12. Functions

12.1 Function Declaration and Calling:

A function in Python is a block of reusable code that performs a specific task. It is defined using the **def** keyword, followed by the function name, parentheses, and a colon. The body of the function is indented and contains the code to be executed when the function is called.

def greet(name):

print(f"Hello, {name}!")

You can call a function by using its name followed by parentheses. Arguments can be passed inside the parentheses if the function expects them.

greet("Alice")

12.2 Parameters and Arguments:

Parameters are placeholders in the function definition, while arguments are the actual values passed to the function when calling it.

def add(x, y):

return x + y

result = add(3, 5) # 3 and 5 are arguments

12.3 Return Statement:

The **return** statement is used to specify the result of a function. It exits the function and returns the specified value or expression.

def multiply(a, b):

*return a * b*

product = multiply(2, 4) # Returns 8

12.4 Default Parameters:

You can assign default values to function parameters. If an argument is not provided, the default value is used.

def power(base, exponent=2):

*return base ** exponent*

result = power(3) # Uses exponent = 2 (default)

12.5 Variable Number of Arguments:

Functions can accept a variable number of arguments using ***args** and ****kwargs**.

*defsum_all(*args):*

total = 0

fornum in args:

total += num

return total

total_sum = sum_all(1, 2, 3, 4) # Sums all arguments

12.6 Lambda Functions (Anonymous Functions):

Lambda functions are small, one-line functions created using the **lambda** keyword.

*square = lambda x: x ** 2*

result = square(5) # Returns 25

12.7 Scope of Variables:

Variables defined within a function are local to that function, while variables defined outside functions have global scope.

x = 10 # Global variable

deffunc():

  y = 5 # Local variable

print(x + y)

func()

12.7 Docstrings:

Docstrings provide documentation for functions, classes, or modules. They describe the purpose, parameters, and return values of a function.

def divide(a, b):

  """""

  Divide two numbers.

:param a: Dividend

:param b: Divisor

:return: Quotient

    """

return a / b

Functions are essential for structuring your code, promoting reusability, and making it easier to manage and understand. They allow you to encapsulate logic, create abstractions, and build modular and maintainable programs.

Note : Args, kwargs required

13. Packages and Modules in Python

In Python, a module is a single file containing Python code. It can include variables, functions, and classes that are related to a specific purpose. Modules are used to organize code and make it more manageable and reusable.

A package, on the other hand, is a collection of related modules. It's essentially a directory containing multiple module files, along with a special __init__.py file that signals to Python that the directory should be treated as a package. Packages provide a way to organize larger projects and break them down into smaller, more focused parts.


```
Windows     ==>  Folder      File
Linux       ==>  Directory   File
P.L Python  ==>  Package     module
```

```
Folder :        all sub folders or

                all files or

                combination of folders and files


Package :       I.  all sub packages or

                II.  all modules or

                 III.  combination of sub packages and modules

module :        Collection of variables, functions and classes

                .py file is a module

list1 = list()

num1 = 10  #int(10)

num2 = -20

print(abs(num1), abs(num2))

builtins.py     - default module available
```

13.1 builtins.py

===============

int

float

bool

string

list

tuple

dict

set

13.2 basics:

----

id() print() input() type()

len() max() min() sorted() sum() range()

help()

enumerate()

filter() map()   reduce() -->functools

abs()   : To get absolute value

all()   :

any()   : The any() function returns True if any item in an iterable are true, otherwise it returns False.

     If the iterable object is empty, the any() function will return False.

any(iterable)

ascii() :

bin()

chr()

dir()

divmod()

eval()

exec()

hash()

ord()

pow()

quit()

13.3 oops:

----

delattr()

getattr()

hasattr()

isinstance() issubclass()

repr()

setattr()

object()

classmethodstaticmethod

classes :int float boolstr list tuple dict set

super

zip

13.4 Exception Handling:

BaseException

Exception

All Errors

ArithmeticError

AttributeError

KeyError

NameError

TypeError

13.5 Iterator :

----

iter() next()

StopIteration

13.6 File Handling:

----

open()

enter()

exit()


```
# from builtins import print, input, len, max, min, print, sorted, sum
print(10)
print("----Builtin function calls-----")
val = input("Enter any number")
print(val)
len()
max()
min()
print()
sorted()
sum()
```


builtins.py

```
# STATE  :builtin data types  -- classes in
#          numbers (intfloat  complex)
#          string list tuple dict set


# Behavior : functions id() input() len() max() min()
#                print()  type()
```

```
#                int() float() long() str() list() tuple() dict() set()
```

Example:

```
list1 = list([1, 2, 3, 4])

print(list1, type(list1), id(list1))

x = 10

list1.append(10)

print(list1, type(list1), id(list1))
```

Examples:

```
 # Generate a random number between 1 to 100

from random import randint

print("Random number : ", randint(100, 200))

# print("Random number : ", random('A', 'Z'))


# Function definition exists in random.py module

# randint(1,100) : function call


# Import string and random module

import string

import random


# Randomly choose a letter from all the ascii_letters

val = random.randint(100, 200)

randomLetter = random.choice(string.ascii_uppercase)

print('Random char :', randomLetter)
```

13.7 Built-ins in Python

- builtins***
- csv***
- datetime**
- json*** json.dumps() json.loads() pickling/unpickling serialization/deserialization
- logging***

- pdb*** Debugging
- pip***
- abc*   : abstract base class used in Abstract Class in OOPs
- asyncio*   :
- base64**   :
- collections* :
- copy*
- http* - sftp https smtp ftp
- importlib
- io*
- ipaddress
- multiprocessing*
- os*
- pickle*
- smtplib
- socket
- sqlite3
- ssl
- subprocess
- threading*
- time*
- timeit*

14. Object Oriented Programming

Why OOPs:

Python is a versatile and multi-paradigm programming language, which means you can write code in a procedural, functional, or object-oriented style.

OOP is often recommended and preferred for various reasons some of them are:

1. **Modularity and Code Reusability**: OOP promotes code organization into classes and objects, which encourages modularity. This makes it easier to understand, maintain, and extend code. You can reuse classes and objects in different parts of your program, leading to more efficient and less error-prone development.

2. **Encapsulation**: OOP allows you to encapsulate data (attributes) and behavior (methods) within objects. This means you can hide the internal state of an object and expose only the necessary interface to interact with it. This reduces the risk of unintended interference with an object's data.

3. **Abstraction**: OOP enables you to create abstract classes and interfaces that define a common set of methods and properties. Subclasses can then inherit from these abstractions and provide specific implementations. This abstraction helps in managing complexity and allows you to work with high-level concepts.

4. **Inheritance**: Inheritance is a key concept in OOP, where a new class (subclass or derived class) can inherit attributes and methods from an existing class (superclass or base class). This promotes code reuse and allows you to model relationships between objects easily.

5. **Polymorphism**: Polymorphism allows objects of different classes to be treated as objects of a common base class. This simplifies code and can make it more flexible. Python supports dynamic typing and polymorphism, making it easy to work with different types of objects in a consistent way.

6. **Maintainability**: OOP promotes well-structured and organized code. This makes it easier to understand, maintain, and extend your codebase over time, which is especially valuable in large projects.

7. **Collaborative Development**: When multiple programmers work on a project, OOP can help divide the work into classes and modules, allowing different team members to focus on specific parts of the code without interfering with each other's work.

Without OOPs:

In the following example the state variable str1 can be accessed and modified by anyone in entire project and solution is , combine both state and behavior and configure in a single entity(i.e, class)

EX: Find length of the string

```
        # 1. STATE
str1 = 'hello world'


        # 2.BEHAVIOR
deffind_length(in_str):
le = 0
for char in in_str:
le += 1
return le


print("Length of string : ", find_length(str1))
str1 = str1 + 'python world'
print("Length of string : ", find_length(str1))
```

Self :

In Python's object-oriented programming (OOP) paradigm, **self** is a special variable that is used within a class definition to refer to the instance of the class itself. It is the first parameter in every instance method of a class and serves as a reference to the object on which the method is called. You can name it anything you like, but by convention, it's named **self** to make code more readable and maintainable.

Here are some key points about **self** in Python OOP:

1. **Instance-specific Data**: When you create an instance (object) of a class, each instance has its own set of attributes (variables) and can have its own unique values for those attributes. **self** allows you to access and manipulate these instance-specific data members within instance methods.

   EX:

```python
classMyClass:
def __init__(self, value):
self.value = value                # 'self' is used to store 'value' as an instance attribute

defdisplay_value(self):
print(self.value)                # 'self' is used to access the instance attribute 'value'

obj1 = MyClass(42)
obj2 = MyClass(100)

obj1.display_value()  # Output: 42
obj2.display_value()  # Output: 100
```

Method Access: When you call an instance method on an object, you don't need to explicitly pass the instance itself as an argument. Python automatically passes the instance as **self** when you make the method call.

EX:

```python
obj1.display_value()  # 'self' refers to 'obj1' inside the display_value method
obj2.display_value()  # 'self' refers to 'obj2' inside the display_value method
```

Access to Other Methods and Attributes: **self** not only allows access to instance attributes but also to other instance methods and attributes within the same class.

EX:

```python
classMyClass:
def __init__(self, value):
self.value = value

defdouble_value(self):
returnself.value * 2

defdisplay_double(self):
```

```python
    doubled = self.double_value()        # Access another method using 'self'
    print(f"Double of {self.value} is {doubled}")


obj = MyClass(5)
obj.display_double()  # Output: Double of 5 is 10
```

Creation of New Attributes: You can use **self** to create new instance attributes dynamically within methods. This allows you to store and manage object-specific data.

EX:

```python
classMyClass:
def __init__(self):
self.data = []  # Create an empty list as an instance attribute


defadd_item(self, item):
self.data.append(item)  # Add an item to the instance-specific list


obj1 = MyClass()
obj2 = MyClass()


obj1.add_item(1)
obj2.add_item(2)


print(obj1.data)  # Output: [1]
print(obj2.data)  # Output: [2]
```

Fields & Methods

A class consists of state and behavior, a state is represented with fields and behavior represented with methods.

A state is collections of fields. Fields are instance variables or class variables.

Methods can be instance methods, class methods or static methods

EX:

```python
class Employee:
                    # Local variables   - eid, name, sal
                    # Instance variables - self.eid self.name self.sal
def __init__(self, eid, name, sal):
self.eid = eid
    self.name = name
self.sal = sal


defget_edata(self):        # Instance Methods
print("Employee information : ", self.eid, self.name, self.sal)
print("value of x : ", x)


print("---Employee-------", Employee)
Obj_1 = Employee(100, "HK, 15000)  # Obj_1 is object
Obj_1.get_edata()
```

Constructor

In Python, a constructor is a special method in a class that is automatically called when an object of the class is created. The constructor method is typically named **__init__** (with double underscores before and after "init"). It is used to initialize the attributes or properties of the object. Constructors are used to ensure that objects of a class are properly initialized and have the necessary attributes to work with. They are an essential part of object-oriented programming in Python.

Defining Constructor

- Default constructor
- Parameterized constructor
    - Positional arguments
    - Default arguments
    - keyword arguments

EX:

```python
class Person:
def __init__(self, name, age):
```

        self.name = name

self.age = age

Creating an instance of the Person class

person1 = Person("Alice", 30)

Accessing the attributes of the object

print(person1.name) # Output: Alice

print(person1.age)   # Output: 30

Default Constructor:

In Python, a default constructor is a constructor that is automatically provided by the Python interpreter when you define a class but don't explicitly provide your own constructor. This default constructor takes no arguments (other than the **self** parameter) and initializes the object with default values for its attributes, if any.

EX1:

class Person:

def __init__(self):

    self.name = "John Doe"

self.age = 0

Creating an instance of the Person class

person1 = Person()

Accessing the attributes of the object

print(person1.name) # Output: John Doe

print(person1.age)   # Output: 0

EX2:

class Employee:

```python
def __init__(self):  # Default constructor
pass  # to perform any generic action


defgetedata(self, eid, sal):
print("Employee Data", eid, sal)
m = Employee()
m.getedata(101, 10000)       # Employee.getedata(m,101,10000)
```

Parameterized Constructor:

 # 1. Positional arguments

```python
class Employee:
    # Parameterized Constructor
def __init__(self, eid, name, sal):
self.eid = eid
    self.name = name
self.sal = sal


defgetedata(self):
pass


Obj = Employee(200, 'HK', 10000)
```

 # 2. Default arguments example

```python
class Employee:
    # parameterized constructors
def __init__(self, eid=None, name=None, sal=None):  # Constructor overloading
self.eid = eid
    self.name = name
self.sal = sal


defgetedata(self):
```

print("Employee info : ", self.eid, self.name, self.sal)

Obj1 = Employee()
Obj1.getedata()

Obj2 = Employee(201)
Obj2.getedata()

Obj1 = Employee(201, 'CS')
Obj1.getedata()

Obj2 = Employee(200, 'Kumar', 10000)
Obj2.getedata()

 # 3. Keyword arguments

farooq = Employee(name='Raja', sal=20000)
farooq.getedata()

Features:

Python supports several Object-Oriented Programming (OOP) features that help you organize and structure your code using objects and classes. Here are some key OOP features in Python:

Classes and Objects:

Python allows you to define classes, which are blueprints for creating objects. Objects are instances of classes.

EX:

class Person:
def __init__(self, name, age):
    self.name = name
self.age = age

person1 = Person("Alice", 30)

Encapsulation:

You can encapsulate data (attributes) and methods (functions) within a class, restricting access to them from outside the class. This is achieved using access modifiers like public, private, and protected (though Python uses name mangling for protected attributes).

EX:

```
class Person:
def __init__(self, name):
self.__name = name  # Private attribute

defget_name(self):  # Getter method
returnself.__name

defset_name(self, name):  # Setter method
self.__name = name

person = Person("Bob")
print(person.get_name())  # Accessing the private attribute using a getter
```

Inheritance: Python supports single and multiple inheritance. You can create new classes that inherit properties and methods from existing classes.

EX:

```
class Student(Person):
def __init__(self, name, age, student_id):
super().__init__(name, age)
self.student_id = student_id
```

Polymorphism: Polymorphism allows you to use different classes in a consistent way. In Python, polymorphism is achieved through method overriding and duck typing.

EX1:

```
defprint_info(person):
print(f"Name: {person.name}")
print(f"Age: {person.age}")
```

```python
person1 = Person("Alice", 30)
student1 = Student("Bob", 20, "12345")


print_info(person1)
print_info(student1)
```

Abstraction: Abstraction allows you to hide complex implementation details and only expose the necessary features of an object.

```python
fromabc import ABC, abstractmethod
```

EX:

```python
class Shape(ABC):
    @abstractmethod
def area(self):
pass


class Circle(Shape):
def __init__(self, radius):
self.radius = radius


def area(self):
return 3.14 * self.radius * self.radius
```

Polymorphism through Duck Typing: Python uses a dynamic typing system where the type of an object is determined at runtime. This allows you to use objects based on their behavior rather than their explicit type.

EX:

```python
defget_area(shape):
returnshape.area()


circle = Circle(5)
square = Square(4)
```

```python
print(get_area(circle))          # Output: 78.5
print(get_area(square))          # Output: 16
```

Access Specifiers :

In Python, access Specifiers are used to control the visibility and accessibility of attributes and methods in a class. Although Python does not have strict access Specifiers like some other programming languages (e.g., Java or C++), it uses naming conventions and a few mechanisms to indicate the level of access for class members. The commonly used access Specifiers in Python are:

Public: In Python, all class members (attributes and methods) are considered public by default. They can be accessed from anywhere, both inside and outside the class.

EX:

```python
classMyClass:
def __init__(self):
self.public_attribute = 42


defpublic_method(self):
return "This is a public method."


obj = MyClass()
print(obj.public_attribute)  # Accessing a public attribute
print(obj.public_method())   # Calling a public method
```

Protected: In Python, protected members are indicated by a single leading underscore before their names. While it's not enforced by the language, it is a convention that suggests to other developers that the member should not be accessed directly from outside the class.

EX:

```python
classMyClass:
def __init__(self):
    self._protected_attribute = 42


def _protected_method(self):
```

return "This is a protected method."

```python
obj = MyClass()
print(obj._protected_attribute)  # Accessing a protected attribute (not recommended)
print(obj._protected_method())   # Calling a protected method (not recommended)
```

Private: Private members are indicated by a double leading underscore before their names. Python enforces name mangling to make it harder to access private members from outside the class. Private members can still be accessed, but it's discouraged.

EX:

```python
classMyClass:
def __init__(self):
    self.__private_attribute = 42

def __private_method(self):
return "This is a private method."

obj = MyClass()
# Accessing private attribute and method (not recommended)
print(obj._MyClass__private_attribute)
print(obj._MyClass__private_method())
```

All Specifiers In one Example

EX:

```python
class Parent:                      # Super class / Parent class / Base class
   clvar1 = "Data"
    _clvar2 = "Qzen"
    __clvar3 = "CRL"
def __init__(self, var1, var2, var3):
    self.var1 = var1
    self._var2 = var2              # Protect variable
```

```python
        self.__var3 = var3                  # Private variable
    def addition(self):                     # Public member function
        print("1. Addition of instance variables is:", self.var1 + self._var2+self.__var3)
    def _addition2(self):                   # Protected Member function
        print("2. Addition of instance variables is:", self.var1 + self._var2+self.__var3)
    def __addition3(self):                  # Private Member function
        print("3. Addition of instance variables is:", self.var1 + self._var2 + self.__var3)


class Child(Parent):                        # Sub class / Child class / Derived class
    defaddition_child(self):
        print("The addition on child class is:", self.var1 + self._var2)


C = Child(10, 23, 33)                       # Child object creation


C.addition_child()
C.addition()                                # Allowed accessing Public member function
C._addition2()                              # Allowed accessing protected member function
#C.__addition3()                            # NOT Allowed accessing private member function
print(C.clvar1)                             # Allowed accessing Public variable
print(C._clvar2)                            # Allowed accessing Protected variable
#print(C.__clvar3)                          # NOT Allowed accessing private variable
```

Output:

The addition on child class is: 33

1. Addition of instance variables is: 66

2. Addition of instance variables is: 66

Data

Qzen

15. Debugging in Python

Debugging in Python is the process of identifying and fixing errors or bugs in your code. Python provides several tools and techniques to help you debug your code effectively. Here are some common methods for debugging in Python:

Print Statements: The simplest debugging technique is to insert print statements in your code to display the values of variables and the flow of execution. You can use the **print()** function to output information at various points in your code to understand what's happening.

EX:

```
defsome_function():
    x = 10
print("Value of x:", x)
    y = x + 5
print("Value of y:", y)
```

Using pdb (Python Debugger): Python has a built-in debugger module called **pdb**. You can use it to step through your code line by line, set breakpoints, and inspect variables interactively. To use **pdb**, import it and insert **pdb.set_trace()** at the point where you want to start debugging:

Run your script, and it will drop you into an interactive debugger prompt where you can type commands like n (next line), c (continue), and p variable (print variable) to inspect and control your code's execution.

EX:

```
importpdb

defsome_function():
    x = 10
pdb.set_trace()  # Start debugging here
    y = x + 5
```

Using IDEs and Text Editors: Many Integrated Development Environments (IDEs) and text editors have built-in debugging tools. Popular choices like PyCharm, Visual Studio Code, and Jupyter Notebook offer debugging capabilities that make it easier to set breakpoints, inspect variables, and step through your code.

Exception Handling: Use try-except blocks to catch and handle exceptions gracefully. This won't help you pinpoint the problem directly, but it will prevent your program from crashing and provide error messages that can give you clues about what went wrong.

```python
try:
    # Code that may raise an exception
except Exception as e:
print("An error occurred:", str(e))
```

Logging: Python's **logging** module allows you to log messages at different levels (e.g., debug, info, warning, error) to help you trace the flow of your program and identify issues.

EX:

```python
import logging
logging.basicConfig(level=logging.DEBUG)
defsome_function():
    x = 10
logging.debug("Value of x: %s", x)
    y = x + 5
logging.debug("Value of y: %s", y)
```

Remember that debugging is often an iterative process. You may need to use a combination of these techniques to identify and fix issues in your code. Additionally, writing clean and modular code with meaningful variable names and comments can make debugging easier and more efficient.

16. Exception Handling

An exception is an event that occurs during the execution of a program and disrupts the normal flow of the program's instructions. Exceptions are typically raised when an error or an unexpected situation occurs in a program. They allow the program to handle and respond to these exceptional conditions gracefully, rather than crashing or producing unpredictable results.

In Python and many other programming languages, exceptions are used to indicate problems such as:

1. **Runtime Errors:** These are errors that occur while the program is running, such as division by zero, attempting to access an element in a list that doesn't exist, or trying to open a file that doesn't exist.

2. **Logical Errors:** These are not necessarily due to exceptional conditions but represent mistakes in the program's logic. For example, incorrect calculations or incorrect program behavior under certain conditions.

3. **User-Defined Errors:** Developers can also create their own custom exceptions to handle specific situations or error cases in their code.

Python provides a wide range of built-in exception types, such as **ZeroDivisionError**, **ValueError**, **TypeError**, **FileNotFoundError**, and many others, each designed to represent a specific type of problem. When an exceptional condition occurs, an exception object is created, and the program flow is transferred to the nearest enclosing **try**block's**except** clause, which can handle the exception or propagate it further up the call stack.

EX:

```
try:
    x = 10 / 0  # This will raise a ZeroDivisionError
exceptZeroDivisionError:
print("An error occurred: Division by zero.")
```

In this code, the division by zero is an exceptional condition that raises a **ZeroDivisionError** exception. The **except** block catches this exception and prints an error message, allowing the program to continue running rather than crashing.

16.1 How to Handle Exceptions:

Exception handling in Python allows you to handle runtime errors or exceptional situations gracefully, preventing your program from crashing. Python provides **try**, **except**, **else**, and **finally** blocks for structured exception handling.

Here's a basic structure for exception handling in Python:

EX:

try:

   # Code that may raise an exception

exceptSomeExceptionType:

   # Code to handle the exception

else:

   # Code to execute if no exception is raised (optional)

finally:

   # Code that always runs, whether an exception occurred or not (optional)

Here's a breakdown of each part of the structure:

1. **try** block: This block contains the code that might raise an exception. If an exception occurs within this block, the program jumps to the corresponding **except** block.

2. **except** block: This block is executed when a specific exception (specified by **SomeExceptionType**) occurs within the **try** block. You can catch and handle the exception here. You can have multiple **except** blocks to handle different types of exceptions.

3. **else** block (optional): This block is executed if no exceptions were raised in the **try** block. It is typically used for code that should run when everything goes smoothly.

4. **finally** block (optional): This block is always executed, regardless of whether an exception occurred or not. It's commonly used for cleanup operations (e.g., closing files or network connections) that should happen no matter what.

EX:

try:

   x = int(input("Enter a number: "))

result = 10 / x

exceptZeroDivisionError:

print("You cannot divide by zero.")

except ValueError:

print("Invalid input. Please enter a valid number.")

else:

print(f"Result: {result}")

finally:

print("Execution complete.")

In above example:

- The **try** block attempts to get user input, convert it to an integer, and perform a division operation.
- If a **ZeroDivisionError** or **ValueError** occurs, the corresponding **except** block is executed.
- If no exception occurs, the **else** block is executed, displaying the result.
- The **finally** block always runs, displaying "Execution complete" at the end.

16.2 Custom Exception Handling : raise

In Python, you can raise an exception using the **raise** statement. An exception is a way to signal that an error or unexpected condition has occurred in your code. You can raise built-in exceptions or create your own custom exceptions.

Here's how to raise an exception in Python:

Raising a Built-in Exception: You can raise one of the many built-in exceptions provided by Python, such as **ValueError**, **TypeError**, **NameError**, or **ZeroDivisionError**. Here's an example:

x = -5

if x < 0:

raiseValueError("x should be a positive number")

In above example, if **x** is less than 0, a **ValueError** exception will be raised with the specified error message.

Raising a Custom Exception: You can also define your custom exceptions by creating a new class that inherits from the built-in **Exception** class or one of its subclasses. Here's an example of how to create and raise a custom exception:

EX:

```python
Class CustomError(Exception):
def __init__(self, message):
super().__init__(message)


defsome_function(x):
if x < 0:
raiseCustomError("x should be a positive number")


try:
some_function(-5)
exceptCustomError as e:
print(f"CustomError raised: {e}")
```

In this example, we define a custom exception **CustomError** and raise it in the **some_function** function when **x** is less than 0.

Raising an Exception with a Cause (Python 3.3+): You can also raise an exception with a specified cause using the **from** keyword. This can be useful for indicating the original cause of an exception:

```python
try:
result = 10 / 0
except ZeroDivisionError as e:
raise ValueError("Error occurred during division") from e
```

In above example, we raise a **ValueError** with the original **ZeroDivisionError** as the cause.

Remember that when raising exceptions, it's essential to provide informative error messages to help you and other developers debug your code effectively. Additionally, it's a good practice to handle exceptions using **try** and **except** blocks to gracefully handle errors and prevent your program from crashing.

17. File Handling

File handling operations in Python are essential for working with files, whether you want to read data from files, write data to files, or manipulate files in other ways. Python provides built-in functions and libraries for performing these operations. Here are some common file handling operations in Python:

Opening a File: You can open a file using the **open()** function. It takes two arguments: the filename and the mode ('r' for reading, 'w' for writing, 'a' for appending, 'b' for binary mode, and more).

EX:

```
# Opening a file for reading
file = open('example.txt', 'r')


# Opening a file for writing (creates a new file if it doesn't exist)
file = open('output.txt', 'w')


# Opening a file in binary mode
file = open('binary.bin', 'rb')
```

Reading from a File: You can read the contents of a file using various methods. The most common method is using the **read()** method.

EX:

```
content = file.read()
```

You can also read the file line by line using a **for** loop:

```
for line in file:
    print(line)
```

Writing to a File: To write data to a file, open it in write ('w') or append ('a') mode and then use the **write()** method.

EX:

```
with open('output.txt', 'w') as file:
    file.write("Hello, World!")
```

Closing a File: It's essential to close a file after you're done with it to release system resources. You can do this explicitly using the **close()** method or by using a **with** statement, which automatically closes the file when you exit the block.

EX:

file.close() # Explicitly closing the file

or

with open('example.txt', 'r') as file:

   # Perform file operations here

File is automatically closed outside the 'with' block

Appending to a File: To append data to an existing file, open it in append ('a') mode and use the **write()** method.

with open('output.txt', 'a') as file:

file.write("Appending new data!")

Checking if a File Exists: You can check if a file exists using the **os.path.exists()** function from the **os** module.

EX:

Import os

ifos.path.exists('example.txt'):

print("File exists.")

else:

print("File does not exist.")

Deleting a File: You can delete a file uşing the **os.remove()** function.

Import os

If os.path.exists('file_to_delete.txt'):

os.remove('file_to_delete.txt')

print("File deleted.")

else:

print("File not found.")

EX: 1 Create a file in append mode , write content onto file and check the file exists or nor.

File open in append mode

file = open("Mani.txt", 'a')

Write content

file.write("\n HAi this is first file")

file.write("\n HAi this is second line")

Check file exists or not

Import os

ifos.path.exists("Rac.txt"):

print("Found File")

else:

print("File not found.")

Create a file to write a string

with open("Mac.txt", "w") as file:

file.write(" I WANT TO PRACTICE CODING.")

EX2: create dynamic list with n-elements and add 10 to each element and write to a file.

L = []

n = int(input("Enter number of elements:"))

forele in range(n):

val = int(input(f"Enter {ele + 1} element:"))

L.append(val)

print("The list is:", L)

Create a list with elements added with a value 10 and written to file

with open("LIST_ELE_SUM_WITH_10.txt", "w") as file:

forele in L:

    s = ele + 10

```python
file.write("\n")
file.write(str(s))
print("FILE UPDATED")
```

EX3:Write a file with factorial values of range each number in a given lower and upper bounds.

```python
# Factorial of n
# n = int(input("Enter a number: "))
def fact(n):
    f = 1
for i in range(1, n + 1):
        f = f * i
return f
#print(f"The factorial of { n } is:", f)

lb = int(input("Enter lb value: "))
ub = int(input("Enter ub value: "))
with open("Fact_result.txt", "w") as file:
for ele in range(lb, ub+1):
        r = fact(ele)
file.write(str(r))
file.write("\n")
print("FILE UPDATED.")
```

18. Decorators

In Python, decorators are a powerful and flexible way to modify or extend the behavior of functions or methods without changing their source code. Decorators are often used to add additional functionality, such as logging, authorization, or validation, to functions or methods. Decorators are themselves functions that take another function as their input and return a new function with the modified behavior. They are typically denoted using the "@" symbol before a function definition.

Here's a basic example of a decorator:

EX:

```python
defmy_decorator(func):
def wrapper():
print("Something is happening before the function is called.")
func()
print("Something is happening after the function is called.")
return wrapper


@my_decorator
defsay_hello():
print("Hello!")


say_hello()
```

In above example, **my_decorator** is a decorator function that takes another function (**func**) as its argument and returns a new function (**wrapper**) that adds behavior before and after the original function is called. When **say_hello** is decorated with **@my_decorator**, calling **say_hello()** will actually call the **wrapper** function, which modifies the behavior of **say_hello** by adding the extra print statements.

Python also provides built-in decorators, and you can create your own custom decorators as well. Some commonly used built-in decorators include **@staticmethod** and **@classmethod**,

EX 1: Add a basic logging feature to a function

```python
deflog_function_call(func):

def wrapper(*args, **kwargs):

print(f"Calling function: {func.__name__}")

result = func(*args, **kwargs)

print(f"{func.__name__} returned: {result}")

return result

return wrapper


@log_function_call

def add(a, b):

return a + b


result = add(3, 5)
```

EX 2: Validate the function using decorators

```python
defvalidate_den(func):

def wrapper(*args, **kwargs):

ifargs[1] == 0:

return "Invalid denominator"

else:

output = func(*args, **kwargs)  # divide(10,2)

return output

return wrapper   # wrapper(10,2)


@validate_den

def divide(n1, n2):

print("-----Divide function-----")

res = n1 / n2

return res

print("Division result : ", divide(10, 0))  # divide (10,2)
```

19. Iterators and Generators

19.1 Iterators:

In Python, an iterator is an object that implements two methods: **__iter__()** and **__next__()**, allowing you to iterate over a collection of items one at a time. Iterators are widely used in Python for looping through sequences of data, such as lists, tuples, dictionaries, and more. Here's how Iterators work in Python:

1. **__iter__() method:**

   - The **__iter__()** method is called when you create an iterator object. It should return the iterator object itself (**self**).

   - This method is necessary to make an object iterable and is typically implemented in a class to define how the iteration should work.

2. **__next__() method:**

   - The **__next__()** method is used to retrieve the next item from the iterator.

   - It should either return the next item or raise a **StopIteration** exception when there are no more items to iterate.

   - You can also use the built-in **next(iterator)** function to get the next item from the iterator.

EX: Custom iterator

```
Class MyIterator:
def __init__(self, start, end):
self.current = start
self.end = end


def __iter__(self):
return self


def __next__(self):
```

```python
ifself.current>= self.end:

raiseStopIteration

else:

self.current += 1

returnself.current - 1


# Using the custom iterator

my_iter = MyIterator(1, 5)


fornum in my_iter:

print(num)
```

In the above example, **MyIterator** is a custom iterator class that allows you to iterate over a range of numbers. The **__next__()** method defines how the iterator generates the next item in the sequence.

EX: Create Iterators using built-in functions like iter() and next() with built-in iterable objects like lists, tuples, and dictionaries.

```python
my_list = [1, 2, 3, 4, 5]
my_iter = iter(my_list)


print(next(my_iter))  # Outputs: 1
print(next(my_iter))  # Outputs: 2
```

In Python, many objects are iterable by default, including strings, lists, tuples, dictionaries, sets, and more. Iterators are a fundamental concept in Python that enables efficient and memory-friendly processing of collections of data.

19.2 Generators

In Python, generators are a type of iterable that allow you to iterate over a potentially large or infinite sequence of items without storing them all in memory at once. They are implemented using functions with one or more **yield** statements.

When you call a generator function, it returns a generator object that you can use to iterate through the values produced by the generator. Generators are particularly useful when working with large datasets or when you want to generate values on-the-fly.

Generator Functions:

- Generator functions are defined like regular functions but use the **yield** keyword to yield values one at a time.
- When a generator function is called, it doesn't execute immediately. Instead, it returns a generator object.
- The state of the generator function is saved, allowing it to resume execution from where it left off when you iterate through the generator.

EX: simple generator function

```python
defsimple_generator():
yield 1
yield 2
yield 3


gen = simple_generator()
for value in gen:
print(value)
```

output:

```
1
2
3
```

Using the next() Function:

- You can use the **next(generator)** function to retrieve the next value produced by the generator.

- When there are no more values to yield, the generator raises a **StopIteration** exception.

EX: Countdown generator function

```python
def countdown(n):
while n > 0:
yield n
    n -= 1


c = countdown(5)
print(next(c))  # Outputs: 5
print(next(c))  # Outputs: 4
print(next(c))  # Outputs: 3
print(next(c))  # Outputs: 2
print(next(c))  # Outputs: 1
```

Generator Expressions:

- In addition to generator functions, Python also supports generator expressions, which are similar to list comprehensions but use parentheses instead of square brackets.
- Generator expressions are a concise way to create simple generators.

EX:

```python
gen = (x for x in range(5))
for value in gen:
print(value)
```

Output:

```
0
1
2
3
4
```

Generators are memory-efficient because they generate values on-the-fly and don't store the entire sequence in memory. They are particularly useful when working with large datasets, streaming data, or when you want to generate values lazily.

20. Date Time

In Python, you can work with dates and times using the **date time** module, which is part of the Python standard library. Here's how you can work with dates and times in Python:

1. Import the **datetime** module:

   importdatetime

2. Get the current date and time:

   current_datetime = datetime.datetime.now()

   print(current_datetime)

3. Get the current date:

   current_date = datetime.date.today()

   print(current_date)

4. Get the current time:

   current_time = datetime.datetime.now().time()

   print(current_time)

5. Create a custom date and time:

   custom_datetime = datetime.datetime(2023, 9, 17, 15, 30, 0) # Year, Month, Day, Hour, Minute, Second

   print(custom_datetime)

6. Extract components of a date or time object:

   year = current_date.year

   month = current_date.month

   day = current_date.day

   hour = current_time.hour

   minute = current_time.minute

   second = current_time.second

7. Format dates and times as strings:

```
formatted_date = current_date.strftime("%Y-%m-%d")

formatted_time = current_time.strftime("%H:%M:%S")

formatted_datetime = current_datetime.strftime("%Y-%m-%d %H:%M:%S")

print(formatted_date)

print(formatted_time)

print(formatted_datetime)
```

8. Parse strings into datetime objects:

```
date_str = "2023-09-17"

parsed_date = datetime.datetime.strptime(date_str, "%Y-%m-%d")

print(parsed_date)
```

9. Perform arithmetic with dates and times:

- You can add or subtract time intervals from datetime objects.

EX:

```
fromdatetime import timedelta

delta = timedelta(days=7)

new_date = current_date + delta

print(new_date)
```

21. Multiprocessing and Threading

Parallel processing and multithreading are techniques used to execute multiple tasks simultaneously in Python. However, Python's Global Interpreter Lock (GIL) can limit the effectiveness of multithreading for CPU-bound tasks. It's important to understand when to use multithreading and when to use multiprocessing based on the nature of tasks.

A process is a program under execution and thread is a light weight process.

It's important to note that due to the Global Interpreter Lock (GIL), Python's threads are limited in their ability to perform true parallel execution for CPU-bound tasks. For such tasks, you should use multiprocessing to take advantage of multiple CPU cores.

For I/O-bound tasks, multithreading is often sufficient and can provide benefits in terms of concurrency. However, if you have a truly CPU-bound task and want to utilize multiple cores, multiprocessing is the way to go.

Remember to be cautious when working with threads or processes that share data, as you may need to use synchronization mechanisms like locks, semaphores, or queues to avoid data corruption and race conditions.

Multiprocessing or Parallel processing:

Multiprocessing is suitable for CPU-bound tasks, as it allows Python to utilize multiple CPU cores. Python's **multiprocessing** module is used for implementing multiprocessing.

EX: split the task of squaring numbers among four processes, making use of multiple CPU cores.

```python
import multiprocessing


defsquare_numbers(numbers, result, index):
fori, num in enumerate(numbers):
result[index + i] = num * num


if __name__ == "__main__":
numbers = [1, 2, 3, 4, 5]
result = multiprocessing.Array("i", len(numbers))
processes = []
```

```python
fori in range(4):  # Use 4 processes
start = i * len(numbers) // 4
end = (i + 1) * len(numbers) // 4
process = multiprocessing.Process(target=square_numbers, args=(numbers[start:end], result, start))
processes.append(process)
process.start()


for process in processes:
process.join()


print(result[:])
```

Multithreading:

Multithreading is useful for tasks that are I/O-bound, such as file I/O, network requests, or waiting for user input. Python's **threading** module is used for implementing multithreading.

EX: Printing numbers and letters by using two threads run concurrently

```python
import threading

defprint_numbers():
fori in range(1, 6):
print(f"Number {i}")


defprint_letters():
for letter in "abcde":
print(f"Letter {letter}")


thread1 = threading.Thread(target=print_numbers)
thread2 = threading.Thread(target=print_letters)


thread1.start()
```

```python
    thread2.start()

    thread1.join()
    thread2.join()

    print("Both threads have finished.")
```

22. Regular expressions

Regular expressions, often referred to as "regex" or "regexp," are powerful tools for pattern matching and text manipulation in Python. Python's re module provides support for working with regular expressions.

- Import the re module:
    - import **re**

We can create a regex pattern using special characters and sequences to define the pattern we want to match.

EX: To match a simple word like "apple," you can create the pattern as follows:

pattern = r"apple"

The **r** before the string denotes a "raw string," which is often used with regex patterns to avoid issues with escaping special characters.

EX: Searching for a match: To search for a match of the pattern in a given string, we can use the re.search() function:

text = "I love apples and oranges."

match = re.search(pattern, text)

if match:

print("Match found:", match.group())

else:

print("No match found")

EX: Matching multiple occurrences: To find all occurrences of the pattern in a string, we can use the re.findall() function:

text = "I have an apple, and she has an apple too."

matches = re.findall(pattern, text)

print("Matches:", matches)

EX: Using regex flags: to perform a case-insensitive search, the re.IGNORECASE flag

pattern = r"apple"

text = "I have an Apple, and she has an APPLE too."

matches = re.findall(pattern, text, re.IGNORECASE)

print("Matches:", matches)

EX: Replacing matched patterns: We can use re.sub() to replace matched patterns with a specified replacement string:

```python
text = "I have an apple, and she has an apple too."
new_text = re.sub(pattern, "orange", text)
print("New text:", new_text)
```

EX: Splitting text using regex: You can split a string into a list using a regex pattern as the delimiter:

```python
text = "apple,banana,cherry,kiwi"
fruits = re.split(r",", text)
print("Fruits:", fruits)
```

EX: Groups and capturing: We can use parentheses () to create groups and capture specific parts of a matched pattern:

```python
pattern = r"(\d{2})-(\d{2})-(\d{4})"
text = "Date of birth: 12-31-2000"
match = re.search(pattern, text)
if match:
day, month, year = match.groups()
print(f"Day: {day}, Month: {month}, Year: {year}")
```

Regular expressions can become quite complex, and there are numerous special characters and techniques available for creating more sophisticated patterns.

Refer: https://docs.python.org/3/library/re.html

23. Networking

Computer networks are organized into layers to provide a structured approach to designing, implementing, and understanding network communication. The most commonly referenced networking model is the **OSI (Open Systems Interconnection) model, which consists of seven layers**. Another widely used model is the **TCP/IP model, which has four or five layers**, depending on the variant. Here, I'll provide an overview of the OSI model and its layers along with their primary uses:

23.1 OSI : 7 –Layers Model

1. Physical Layer:

- **Function**: It deals with the physical medium, such as cables, switches, and network interface cards (NICs).
- **Uses**: Transmit raw bits over a physical medium, define physical characteristics (e.g., voltage levels), and manage data transmission rates.

2. Data Link Layer:

- **Function**: It focuses on creating a reliable link between two directly connected nodes (e.g., switches, bridges).
- **Uses**: Frame synchronization, error detection and correction (e.g., Ethernet frames), MAC address assignment, and flow control.

3. Network Layer:

- **Function**: Responsible for routing packets between different networks and subnets.
- **Uses**: IP (Internet Protocol) addressing, routing (e.g., IPv4, IPv6), logical addressing, and packet forwarding.

4. Transport Layer:

- **Function**: Ensures end-to-end communication, reliability, and data segmentation/reassembly.
- **Uses**: TCP (Transmission Control Protocol) for reliable and connection-oriented communication, UDP (User Datagram Protocol) for connectionless communication, port numbers, and error checking.

5. Session Layer:

- **Function**: Manages sessions (connections) between applications running on different devices.
- **Uses**: Session establishment, maintenance, and termination; dialog control; and synchronization.

6. Presentation Layer:

- **Function**: Deals with data translation, encryption, and compression to ensure that data is in a readable format.
- **Uses**: Data encryption/decryption, character encoding/decoding (e.g., ASCII, UTF-8), and data compression.

7. Application Layer:

- **Function**: The topmost layer that interacts directly with end-user applications.
- **Uses**: Provides network services directly to applications (e.g., HTTP for web browsing, SMTP for email, FTP for file transfer).

23.2 TCP/IP: 4 – Layers Models

1. Link Layer:

- **Function**: Combines elements of the OSI Physical and Data Link layers.
- **Uses**: Frames and link-specific addressing (e.g., MAC addresses).

2. Internet Layer:

- **Function**: Combines the Network layer of OSI.
- **Uses**: IP addressing, routing (IPv4 and IPv6).

3. Transport Layer:

- **Function**: Similar to the OSI Transport layer.
- **Uses**: End-to-end communication, flow control, and error checking (TCP and UDP).

4. Application Layer:

- **Function**: Corresponds to the OSI Application layer.
- **Uses**: Application-specific protocols and services.

Each layer of these models has a distinct purpose and plays a crucial role in enabling communication across networks. By breaking down network functions into layers, it becomes easier to design, troubleshoot, and replace specific components of a network without affecting the entire system.

23.3 Networking in Python:

Networking in Python involves using libraries and modules to create, manage, and interact with network connections, whether it's for sending and receiving data over the internet, communicating with other devices on a local network, or building network applications.

Python provides several built-in and third-party libraries for networking tasks. Here are some key libraries and concepts to get you started:

Socket Programming: Python's **socket** library is the foundation for network communication. It allows to create sockets and work with various socket types, such as TCP and UDP.

EX: Create a TCP server and client using sockets:

```python
# Server
import socket
server_socket = socket.socket(socket.AF_INET, socket.SOCK_STREAM)
server_socket.bind(("0.0.0.0", 12345))
server_socket.listen(5)

while True:
client_socket, addr = server_socket.accept()
data = client_socket.recv(1024)
print(f"Received data: {data.decode()}")
client_socket.close()


# Client
import socket

client_socket = socket.socket(socket.AF_INET, socket.SOCK_STREAM)
client_socket.connect(("server_ip", 12345))
client_socket.send(b"Hello, server!")
client_socket.close()
```

Requests Library: The **requests** library is excellent for making HTTP requests. It simplifies working with RESTful APIs and web services.

EX: Create HTTP requests

```python
import requests
response = requests.get("https://jsonplaceholder.typicode.com/posts/1")
print(response.status_code)
print(response.json())
```

Twisted: Twisted is an event-driven networking engine for building networked applications. It supports protocols like TCP, UDP, SSL, and more. It's suitable for building servers, clients, and custom network protocols.

EX: Create Custom protocols

```python
fromtwisted.internet import protocol, reactor

classMyProtocol(protocol.Protocol):
defconnectionMade(self):
self.transport.write(b"Hello, client!")

defdataReceived(self, data):
print(f"Received data from client: {data}")

classMyFactory(protocol.Factory):
defbuildProtocol(self, addr):
returnMyProtocol()

reactor.listenTCP(12345, MyFactory())
reactor.run()
```

Asyncio: The **asyncio** library provides a framework for asynchronous programming, making it useful for building asynchronous network applications, such as web servers and clients.

EX: Asynchronous programming

```python
importasyncio
```

```python
asyncdeffetch_url(url):
async with aiohttp.ClientSession() as session:
async with session.get(url) as response:
return await response.text()


asyncdef main():
url = "https://jsonplaceholder.typicode.com/posts/1"
data = await fetch_url(url)
print(data)


asyncio.run(main())
```

Networking Libraries: There are various third-party libraries tailored for specific network tasks.For example, **aiohttp** for building asynchronous HTTP clients and servers, **paramiko** for SSH, and **pySNMP** for SNMP (Simple Network Management Protocol) operations.

Remember to install any third-party libraries using **pip** before using them in your Python code. Networking in Python can be a complex topic, depending on your specific use case, so it's essential to refer to the official documentation and tutorials for each library or module you plan to use.

24. Web Scraping

Web scraping is the process of automatically extracting information from websites. It involves retrieving and parsing HTML or other structured data from web pages and then extracting specific pieces of information for various purposes, such as data analysis, research, or data integration into other applications.

Web scraping is typically used when the desired data is not available through APIs (Application Programming Interfaces) or when APIs are not provided by the website owner. It allows users to collect data from websites by programmatically simulating human interactions with a web browser, such as clicking links and submitting forms, and then extracting data from the resulting web pages.

Here are some key components and concepts related to web scraping:

1. **HTTP Requests**: Web scraping begins with sending HTTP requests to the target website's server. This request asks the server to return the contents of a specific web page.

2. **HTML Parsing**: Once the web page is retrieved, the HTML content is parsed to extract the structured information it contains. This is often done using libraries like BeautifulSoup in Python.

3. **Data Extraction**: After parsing the HTML, web scrapers identify and extract the desired data from the web page, such as text, tables, images, links, or specific elements with certain attributes.

4. **Data Storage**: Extracted data can be stored in various formats, such as CSV, JSON, or a database, depending on the project's requirements.

5. **Automation**: Web scraping can be automated using scripts or programs, which can navigate through multiple pages, follow links, and repeat the extraction process for a large volume of data.

6. **Respect for Terms of Service**: It's essential to respect the terms of service and legal considerations of the website you are scraping. Some websites may prohibit scraping in their terms, while others may offer APIs for accessing their data.

Web scraping is a powerful tool but should be used responsibly and ethically. Some websites have security measures in place to detect and block web scrapers, so developers may need to implement techniques like rate limiting and user-agent spoofing to avoid detection and ensure the reliability of their web scraping processes.

24.1 Python Web scraping Process :

Web scraping in Python can be accomplished using various libraries, but one of the most popular and powerful libraries for web scraping is**BeautifulSoup** in combination with **Requests**.

1. **Install Required Libraries**: Before you start, you need to install the necessary libraries if you haven't already. You can use **pip** to install them:

   pip install requests beautifulsoup4

2. **Import Libraries**: In your Python script, import the required libraries:

   import requests

   from bs4 import BeautifulSoup

3. **Send HTTP Request**: Use the **requests** library to send an HTTP GET request to the website you want to scrape.

   url = 'https://example.com'

   response = requests.get(url)

   # Check if the request was successful

   ifresponse.status_code == 200:

       # Parse the HTML content of the page

   soup = BeautifulSoup(response.text, 'html.parser')

   else:

   print('Failed to retrieve the page')

4. **Parse HTML Content**: With BeautifulSoup, you can navigate and search the HTML structure of the page to find and extract the data you need. You can use various methods, such as **find(), find_all()**, and CSS selectors, to locate elements on the page.

   # Find a specific element by its tag and attributes

   element = soup.find('tag_name', {'attribute_name': 'attribute_value'})

```python
# Find all elements with a specific class
elements = soup.find_all('tag_name', class_='class_name')

# Extract text from an element
text = element.get_text()

# Access attributes of an element
attribute_value = element['attribute_name']
```

5. **Data Extraction and Processing**: Once we have located the elements containing the data want to scrape, extract and process the data as needed. we can store it in variables, lists, or data structures for further use.

6. **Iterating and Pagination**: For web pages with multiple items or paginated content, we may need to iterate through pages by sending additional requests and repeating the parsing process.

7. **Data Storage**: Depending on your project's requirements, we can store the scraped data in various formats, such as CSV, JSON, or a database.

8. **Handling Errors and Exceptions**: Implement error handling to deal with situations where web pages may not load correctly or expected elements are missing.

9. **Respect Robots.txt**: Always respect the website's **robots.txt** file, which can specify rules and restrictions for web crawlers and scrapers. Avoid scraping pages that are explicitly disallowed.

10. **Rate Limiting**: Implement rate limiting to avoid overloading the target website's server with too many requests in a short period.

25. Database Access

Database access is a fundamental aspect of modern software development and data management, enabling efficient and secure data storage, retrieval, and manipulation across a wide range of industries and applications. The choice of database system and the methods for accessing it depend on the specific needs and requirements of the project or application.

Python provides several libraries and modules for accessing and interacting with databases. You can use these libraries to connect to databases, execute SQL queries, and retrieve or manipulate data.

Some of the commonly used libraries for database access in Python include:

1. **SQLite (Built-in)**: SQLite is a lightweight, built-in database system in Python. It doesn't require a separate server and is ideal for small to medium-sized applications.

```python
import sqlite3

# Connect to a SQLite database or create one if it doesn't exist
conn = sqlite3.connect("mydatabase.db")

# Create a cursor object to execute SQL queries
cursor = conn.cursor()

# Execute SQL queries
cursor.execute("CREATE TABLE IF NOT EXISTS users (id INTEGER PRIMARY KEY, name TEXT)")

# Insert data
cursor.execute("INSERT INTO users (name) VALUES (?)", ("John",))

# Commit changes and close the connection
conn.commit()
conn.close()
```

2. **MySQL and MariaDB**: we can use the **mysql-connector-python** library to interact with MySQL and MariaDB databases.

```python
importmysql.connector

# Connect to the database
conn = mysql.connector.connect(
host="localhost",
user="username",
```

```python
password="password",
database="mydb"
)

# Create a cursor
cursor = conn.cursor()

# Execute SQL queries
cursor.execute("SELECT * FROM users")
rows = cursor.fetchall()

# Close the connection
conn.close()
```

3. **PostgreSQL**: The **psycopg2** library is commonly used to work with PostgreSQL databases.

```python
import psycopg2

# Connect to the database
conn = psycopg2.connect(
host="localhost",
user="username",
password="password",
database="mydb"
)

# Create a cursor
cursor = conn.cursor()

# Execute SQL queries
cursor.execute("SELECT * FROM users")
rows = cursor.fetchall()

# Close the connection
conn.close()
```

4. **MongoDB (NoSQL)**: For NoSQL databases like MongoDB, you can use the **pymongo** library.

```python
frompymongo import MongoClient

# Connect to MongoDB
```

```python
client = MongoClient("mongodb://localhost:27017/")

# Access a database
db = client["mydb"]

# Access a collection
collection = db["mycollection"]

# Insert a document
collection.insert_one({"name": "Alice"})

# Find documents
results = collection.find({"name": "Alice"})
# Close the connection
client.close()
```

5. **Object-Relational Mapping (ORM)**: Libraries like SQLAlchemy and Django ORM provide a higher-level, object-oriented way to interact with databases, making it easier to work with relational databases.

```python
fromsqlalchemy import create_engine, Column, Integer, String
fromsqlalchemy.orm import sessionmaker
fromsqlalchemy.ext.declarative import declarative_base

# Define a database model
Base = declarative_base()

class User(Base):
    __tablename__ = "users"
id = Column(Integer, primary_key=True)
name = Column(String)

# Create an SQLite database engine
engine = create_engine("sqlite:///mydatabase.db")

# Create tables
Base.metadata.create_all(engine)

# Create a session
Session = sessionmaker(bind=engine)
session = Session()
```

```python
# Insert data
new_user = User(name="Bob")
session.add(new_user)
session.commit()

# Query data
users = session.query(User).all()
for user in users:
    print(user.name)

# Close the session
session.close()
```

26. Flask – Web Framework (Micro services)

Flask is a lightweight and versatile web framework for building web applications and APIs in Python. It's known for its simplicity and flexibility, making it an excellent choice for developers who want to create web applications quickly and efficiently. Here's an overview of Flasbk and how to get started:

26.1 Key Features:

1. **Micro Framework**: Flask is a micro framework, which means it provides only the essentials for building web applications. This simplicity allows developers to choose and integrate additional libraries and components as needed.

2. **Routing**: Flask allows you to define URL routes and associate them with functions (views) that handle requests. This makes it easy to create the various pages and endpoints of your web application.

3. **HTTP Methods**: You can define routes that respond to different HTTP methods (GET, POST, PUT, DELETE, etc.), allowing you to create RESTful APIs and handle form submissions.

4. **Template Engine**: Flask includes Jinja2, a powerful template engine, for rendering HTML pages. It enables you to separate the presentation layer from your Python code.

5. **Extensions**: Flask has a rich ecosystem of extensions that provide additional functionality, such as database integration (SQLAlchemy, Flask-SQLAlchemy), authentication (Flask-Login, Flask-Principal), and more.

6. **Werkzeug and Jinja2**: Flask is built on top of two powerful libraries: Werkzeug for handling HTTP requests and responses, and Jinja2 for rendering templates. These libraries provide the foundation for Flask's functionality.

26.2 Project Structure:

Creating a well-structured project in Flask is essential for maintaining a clean and organized codebase. While there's no single "right" way to structure a Flask project, I can provide you with a common project structure that you can use as a starting point. You can always customize it to fit your specific needs as your project grows.

```
project_name/
├── app/
│   ├── __init__.py
│   ├── routes/
│   │   ├── __init__.py
│   │   ├── auth.py              # Authentication-related routes
│   │   ├── main.py              # Main application routes
│   │   └── ...
│   ├── models.py               # Database models (if using a database)
│   ├── templates/              # HTML templates
│   ├── static/                 # Static files (CSS, JavaScript, images)
│   └── ...
├── config.py                   # Configuration settings
├── venv/                       # Virtual environment (create using virtual
├── requirements.txt            # List of project dependencies
├── run.py                      # Application entry point
└── README.md                   # Project documentation
```

Here's a brief explanation of each component:

1. **app/**: This is the core of your Flask application.

    - **__init__.py**: Initializes the Flask application and sets up various extensions (if any).

    - **routes/**: A package containing your application's routes.

        - **__init__.py**: Initializes the routes package.

        - **auth.py**: Contains routes related to user authentication (e.g., login, registration).

        - **main.py**: Contains the main application routes (e.g., homepage, user profile).

        - You can create more route files as needed.

    - **models.py** (optional): Defines your database models if you're using a database with Flask (e.g., SQLAlchemy).

    - **templates/**: Store your HTML templates here.

    - **static/**: Store static files like CSS, JavaScript, and images here.

    - Other necessary packages or modules specific to your application.

2. **config.py**: Configuration settings for your application, such as database URLs, secret keys, and other settings. You can separate configurations for development, production, and testing environments.

3. **venv/**: This is a virtual environment directory where you can create and manage your Python environment using tools like **virtualenv** or Python's built-in **venv**.

4. **requirements.txt**: A text file listing all the Python packages and their versions required for your project. You can generate this file using **pip freeze** or similar tools.

5. **run.py**: The entry point for your Flask application. It typically contains the code to create and run the Flask app instance.

6. **README.md**: Project documentation that explains how to set up and run your project, its purpose, and any other relevant information.

26.3 Python App Development:

- **Installation**: First, you need to install Flask using **pip**:

  - pip install Flask

- **Creating a Basic Flask App**: Here's a minimal example of a Flask application:

```
from flask import Flask
app = Flask(__name__)
@app.route('/')
def hello():
return 'Hello, World!'
if __name__ == '__main__':
app.run(debug=True)
```

- **Running the App**: Save the code in a Python file (e.g., **app.py**) and run it: You'll see output indicating that the Flask development server is running. You can access the application in your web browser at http://localhost:5000.

  - python app.py

- **Routes and Views**: Define additional routes and views by creating functions and using the **@app.route** decorator. These functions handle HTTP requests and return responses.

- **Templates**: Create HTML templates using Jinja2 to render dynamic content. Flask allows to pass data from your views to templates for rendering.

- **Static Files**: Store static files like CSS, JavaScript, and images in a folder (e.g., **static**) within project directory. Flask can serve these files using the **url_for** function in templates.

- **Database Integration**: If application requires database functionality, you can integrate Flask with various database systems using extensions like Flask-SQLAlchemy (for SQLAlchemy) or Flask-MongoEngine (for MongoDB).

- **Deployment**: When application is ready for production, you can deploy it on various platforms, including traditional web hosts, cloud services, or containerized solutions like Docker.

27. Technical Interview Questions – Practice

Introduction:

===========

0. Introduce yourself.

1. Tell me about Python?

2. Why Python is so popular now a days?

3. Features of Python

4. Advantages and Disadvantages of Python

5. Interpreted vs Compiled time programming languages. Explain in detail

6. .py vs .pyc files

7. How compilation will happen internally. Explain in detail

8. Why Python is Dynamically typed programming Language. Explain

9. Python is Platform independent. Explain

10. Different ways to write python program.

   Interactive, IDLE, Command Prompt, IDE

   Advantages, Disadvantages

Variables:

========

1. x = 10. Explain in detail for CRUD operations

2. tokens in Python. Explain all types

3. Garbage collection. How it works internally

4. Memory Management in Python

5. Dynamically typed programming. Explain examples.

6. Initializing variable, static, dynamic way

7. Assigning value to multiple variables. Explain

IDE PyCharm:

===========

1. Different IDEs in market

2. Advantages of IDE

3. Shortcuts in PyCharm (Explain min 10)

Operators:

=========

1. Explain in detail about all operators

2. == vs is

3. and or operators. Explain 2 examples

4. Operator precedence.

5. Subtract 2 numbers and print result program.

     - Write down all scenarios with different input values

Data Types:

==========

1. Importance of DataTypes.2

2. Different data types, data structures available in Python

3. int vs float

4. Boolean. give all scenarios

5. 0 vs null

6. Explain each data type, data structure with real life examples.

7. CRUD Operations. Give examples for each

8. Sequences. Types of sequences. Sequence operations

9. Explain about below functions and give examples

    print()

    id()

    type()

    int()

    float()

    complex()

    bool()

    input()

Keyword:

========

1. Explain all keywords with examples and areas of usage

Decision Making:

==============

1. What is Decision Making. Explain different scenarios when to go for Decision Making

2. Give examples for below conditions

    1. single if :

    2. if else:

    3. if elif else:

    4. if elif elif else:

    5. Nested if:

3. Prepare Programs for below questions

    1. Prepare state and assign North South West East

    north = []

        south = ['Andhra Prades', 'Telangana', 'Karnataka','Tamil Nadu', 'Kerala']

        west = []

        east = []

    2. Prepare dictionary with key as state name and value as "list of districts"

4. Get employee details(in dict format, empid,name,sal, exp) and update hike for employee with below

        If exp is 0 to 2 years - 10% Hike

                2 to 5 years - 20% Hike

                5 to 8 years - 30% Hike

                8+   - No hike

5. Explain below terms in detail

    - Requirement

    - User Criteria

    - Validations(Client vs Server)

6. State vs Behavior . Examples

Loops:

======

1. Importance of Loops

2. while loop. Explain in detail with different use cases

3. for loop. Explain in detail with different use cases

4. while vs for

5. Give examples while with if else combination

6. Give examples for with if else combination

7. Control statements. Explain and give examples for each keyword

   - break

   - continue

   - pass

8. Implement 5 examples which covers all topics if elif else for while break/continue/pass

Data Structures:

==============

    1. What are CRUD operations. Explain in detail

    2. Sequence. Types. Operations on each sequence

    3. HTTP Request methods for CRUD. Explain in detail

  i. Numbers:

    1. Types of numbers. Explain each use case

    2. type conversions

    3. Explain different operations of Boolean type

  ii. String:

    1. Explain about string.

    2. Multi line string

    3. String is Immutable. Explain in detail

    4. CRUD Operations on String

    5. Sequence operations on String

6. Memory allocation of String

7. Explain 10 important functions of String

iii. List:

1. What is use of list. Explain different use cases of List

2. Sequence operations on List

3. Characteristics(Properties) of List

4. CRUD operations on List

5. Memory allocation of List

6. Write all possible combinations of list structure(homo, hetero with all data types, data structures)

7. Explain about each method of List

   append:

   pop:

   ....

8. shallow copy vs deep copy

9. append vs extend

10. pop vs remove

11. Pass by value vs Pass by reference

iv. Tuple:

1. What is use of Tuple. Explain different use cases of Tuple

2. Sequence operations on Tuple

3. Characteristics(Properties) of Tuple

4. CRUD operations on Tuple

5. Memory allocation of Tuple

6. Write all possible combinations of Tuple structure(homo,hetero with all data types, data structures)

7. Explain about each function of Tuple

8. shallow copy vs deep copy in tuple.

9. list vs tuple (Min. 4 differences in detail)

v. Dictionary:

1. Dictionary real-time usage scenarios

2. Properties of Dictionary. Explain in detail

3. Dictionary methods

4. Dictionary is mutable or immutable. Why

5. Explain in dictionary function

6. Hashing algorithm in dictionary

vi. Set:

1. Properties of Set

2. Functions of Set

Functions:

=========

1. What is a function

2. Why we need to write functions

3. Define function and explain in detail

4. State vs Behavior

5. Function types

6. Function calling ways

7. How to print function name. Explain how a function will be loaded

8. Parameter vs Argument

9. Variable vs Value

10. Different ways of calling function

11. Function overloading

12. Anonymous function. Explain in detail

13. Lambda with map filter and reduce functions. Explain in detail with examples

14. Function memory allocation

15. Scope of variable. Explain about LEGB rule

Packages, Modules:

=================

1. Importance of Package vs Module

2. file vs module

3. package vs module

4. Builtin libraries. Explain about min 10 libraries in python

5. from import vs import (Directly importing module vs importing specific function/class from module)

6. Create 2 packages, modules inside it. Call function from first package inside second package module

7. __init__.py file in each package. Why. Importance

10. if __name__ == '__main__': What it means ?

OOPs:

=====

1. What is OOPs

2. Why OOPs required

3. Features of OOPs

4. class vs object

5. class vs instance vs local variables. Explain in detail about usecase of each variable

6. class vs instance vs static method. Explain in detail about usecase of each Method

7. Importance of init method

8. Importance of self

9. object life cycle

10. Constructor. Explain in detail

11. Constructor life cycle

12. Default vs Parameterized Constructor

13. Constructor Overloading

14. new vs init

15. Explain below concepts in detail with examples

    a. Encapsulation

    b. Abstraction

    c. Inheritance

    d. Polymorphism

16. Method overloading vs Method overriding

17. Inheritance types

18. MRO principle.Explain in detail

19. Access modifiers in Python

20. Multiple Inheritance. Explain in detail

21. super keyword importance

22. Calling super class method from sub class

23. Difference between public protected private methods Ex: x() _x() __x()

24. Importance of dunder functions

25. __str__ vs __repr__

26. Abstraction, Abstract class. When to use. Explain in detail

27. Abstract class vs Interface

Debugging:

==========

1. Importance of debugging

2. Debugging shortcuts(F6,F5...)

3. pdb module

4. pdb module commands

Exception Handling:

=================

1. Importance of Exception handling

2. error vs exception

3. Different exception classes used in your project

4. try vs except vs else vs finally. Explain in detail

5. Exception order while defining in except blocks

6. Multiple ways of writing except blocks

7. How to create and raise custom exception

File Handling:

==========

1. Importance of file

2. Different files in general

3. File open modes

4. How to work with files. Open read/write/append Close. Give examples

5. Importance of context manager. Explain in detail

6. enter vs exit

7. Who to open text,csv,excel,pdf,image,audio,video,jpeg using open and with statements

28. Coding Challenges – Interview Practice

FUNCTIONS CODING CHALLENGES

1   check given word is palindrome or not

```python
def palindrome(word):
  if word == word[::-1]:
    print("PALINDROME")
  else:
    print("NOT A PALINDROME")


wrd = input("enter a word:")
palindrome(wrd)
```

2   print even and odd numbers

```python
def even1(n):
  print(list(x for x in range(n) if x % 2 == 0))
def odd1(n):
  print(list(y for y in range(n) if y % 2 == 1))


num = int(input("Enter range value:"))
print("Even NUMS:")
even1(num)
print("ODD NUMS:")
odd1(num)
```

3   print prime numbers

```python
def chkprime(x):
  c = 0
  for i in range(2, x):
    if x % i == 0:
      c += 1
  if c == 0:
    return True
  else:
    return False


def prime(n):
```

```python
    for num in range(2, n+1):
        if chkprime(num) == True:
            print(num, end=' ')

if __name__ == '__main__':
    r = int(input("Enter a number range:"))
    prime(r)
```

4   factorial of given number

```python
def fact(n):
    if n == 0 or n == 1:
        return 1
    else:
        return n * fact(n-1)

num = int(input("Enter number:"))
f = fact(num)
print("The factorial of {} is: ".format(num), f)
```

5   convert list/tuple/set to list/tuple/set

```python
L = [1, 3, 44, 5]
print("List-->", L)
print("Tuple-->", tuple(L))
print("Set-->", set(L))
```

6   find cube/square of a number

```python
num = int(input("Enter a number:"))
print("SQUARE IS:", num * num)
print("CUBE IS:", num * num * num)
```

7   table of the given number

```python
num = int(input("Enter a number:"))
for i in range(1, 11):
    print(num, '*', i, '=', num * i)
```

8   find the Max of three numbers

```python
num1 = int(input("Enter 1st num:"))
num2 = int(input("Enter 2nd num:"))
num3 = int(input("Enter 3rd num:"))
if num3 > num1 and num3 > num2:
    print(' 3rd number {} is BIGGER'.format(num3))
elif num2 > num3 and num2 > num1:
    print('2nd number {} is BIGGER'.format(num2))
elif num1 > num3 and num1 > num2:
    print('1st number {} is BIGGER'.format(num1))
elif num3 == num1 and num1 == num2:
    print('ALL ARE EQUAL')
```

9   Fibonacci series?

```python
n1 = 0
n2 = 1
n3 = 1
R = 10
print("Fibonacci series with {} numbers are:".format(R))
print(n1, n2, n3, end=' ')
C = 3
while C != R:
    n4 = n3 + n2
    print(n4, end=' ')
    C += 1
    n3, n2 = n4, n3
```

10   sum all the numbers in a list

```python
import random
L = [random.randint(1, 7) for i in range(10)]
print("The given list is:", L)
print("The sum of elements of list:", sum(L))
print("The multiplications of list elements:", end=' ')
m = 1
for ele in L:
    m = m * ele
print(m)
```

11   multiply all the numbers in a list

```python
import random
L = [random.randint(1, 7) for i in range(10)]
print("The given list is:", L)
print("The sum of elements of list:", sum(L))
print("The multiplications of list elements:", end=' ')
m = 1
for ele in L:
    m = m * ele
print(m)
```

12   to reverse a string

```python
str1 = "hai this is hanuman"
print("The reverse of given string is:", str1[::-1])
```

13   check whether a number is in a given range

```python
st = int(input("Enter start:"))
ed = int(input("Enter end:"))
num = int(input("Enter number to check in range:"))
if num > st and num < ed:
    print("{} is in range of ({} , {})".format(num, st, ed))
else:
    print("{} is not in range of ({} , {})".format(num, st, ed))
```

14   accepts a string and calculate the number of upper case letters and lower case letters

```python
str1 = 'Hello PLease COmeKKo'
U = 0
L = 0
for char in str1:
    if char.isupper():
        U += 1
    elif char.islower():
        L += 1
print("The Upper char count is ", U)
print("The Lower char count is ", L)
```

15   takes a list and returns a new list with unique elements of the first list.

```python
L = [11, 22, 11, 34, 25, 27, 22, 34]
print("Given list:", L)
print("The Unique elements list:", list(set(L)))
```

16   print the even numbers from a given list

```python
L = [11, 22, 33, 44, 55, 6]
for ele in L:
    if ele % 2 == 0:
        print(ele)
```

17   print given Pascal's triangle

```python
def fact(n):
    if n == 0 or n == 1:
        return 1
    else:
        return n * fact(n-1)


rows = int(input("enter number of rows:"))
for i in range(rows):
    for space in range(rows-i + 1):
        print(end=' ')

    for j in range(i+1):
        print(fact(i)//(fact(j)*fact(i-j)), end=' ')

    print()
```

18   function to display group of strings

```python
L = ["Hai", 22, 43, 'Hak', 'Hel', 22, 44]
for ele in L:
    if type(ele) == str:
        print(ele)
```

19   function to check whether a string is a pangram or not

```python
str1 = input("Enter string:")
if str1 == str1[::-1]:
```

```python
    print("PALINDROME")
else:
    print("NOT A PALINDROME")
```

20   to match the item in two dictionaries.

```python
dict1 = {'A': 1, 'B': 2, 'C': 3}
dict2 = {'B': 2, 'A': 1, 'C': 3}
if dict1 == dict2:
    print("EQUAL")
else:
    print("NOT EQUAL")
```

STRINGS: (3 – ways of Implementation)

1   Length of string

```python
str1 = input("Enter string to find length: ")
print("1. With built in: ")
print("Length of string is:", len(str1))

print("2. Without built in: ")
l = 0
for char in str1:
    l += 1
print("Length of string is:", l)

print("3. With function:")

def len_fun(str_):
    print("Length of string is:", len(str1))

len_fun(str1)
```

2   Count characters in string

```python
str1 = input("Enter string to count chars:")
dict1 = {}
for i in str1:
```

```python
    dict1[i] = str1.count(i)
print("I Method- The chars count in given string: ", dict1)

import  collections
print("II Method-The chars count in given string:", collections.Counter(str1))

def char_count(str1):
    dict1 = {}
    for i in str1:
        dict1[i] = str1.count(i)
    print("III Method- The chars count in given string: ", dict1)
char_count(str1)
```

3   String slicing

```python
str1 = input("Enter a string:")
print("I. With builtin String slice-->:",str1[0:3])
print("II. Without builtin-->:", end='')
for c in range(3):
    print(str1[c], end='')
print("\nIII. With function--->:", end='')

def str_slice(str1):
    for c in range(3):
        print(str1[c], end='')

str_slice(str1)
```

4   Replace first occurrence character

```python
str1 = input("Enter a string: ")
char = input("which char you want to replace: ")
new_str = str1.replace(char, '*', 1)
print('I- BuiltIn Method Replaced string:', new_str)
new_str = ""
count = 0
for c in str1:
    if c != char:
        new_str = new_str + c
    elif count == 0 and c == char:
        new_str = new_str + '*'
```

```python
        count += 1
    else:
      new_str = new_str + c
print("II-Without Method Replaced string", new_str)
def replace_1st(str1, char):
   new_str = str1.replace(char, '*', 1)
   print('III- Function Replaced string:', new_str)
replace_1st(str1, char)
```

5   Swapping chars in string

```python
str1 = input("Enter  a string: ")
p1, p2 = int(input('Enter positions1: ')), int(input("Enter position2 to swap: "))

l = list(str1)
l[p1], l[p2] = l[p2], l[p1]
new_str = " "
# print(l)
for i in l:
   new_str += i

print("II. Without builtin The Swapped String: ", new_str)

def swap_function(str1, p1, p2):
   l = list(str1)
   l[p1], l[p2] = l[p2], l[p1]
   new_str1 = " "
   # print(l)
   for i in l:
      new_str1 += i
   print("III. With Function The Swapped String: ", new_str1)
swap_function(str1, p1, p2)
```

6   Append chars to string at end

```python
str1 = input("Enter string: ")
chars = input("Enter chars to append: ")
new_str = str1 + chars
print("Before append: ", str1)
print("II without builtin After append: ", new_str)
```

```python
def append_chars(str1, chars):
    list1 = list(str1)
    list1.append(chars)
    print("III Function After append:", "".join(list1))
append_chars(str1, chars)
```

7   Substring replacement

```python
str1 = input("Enter a string: ")
sub_str = input("Enter substring to replace: ")
position = int(input("Enter position to replace: "))
l = list(str1)
l.insert(position, sub_str)
new_str = "".join(l)
print("The string before replacement: ", str1)
print("II Without builtIn the string after replacement: ", new_str)


def sub_replace(str1, sub_str, position):
    list1 = list(str1)
    list1[position] = sub_str
    print("III Function :", "".join(list1))
sub_replace(str1, sub_str, position)
```

8   Length of longest string in python

```python
str1 = input("Enter the string:")
L = str1.split(" ")

len_list = []
for i in L:
    len_list.append(len(i))
for val in L:
    if len(val) == max(len_list):
        print("I Method- The longest string is: ", val)

s = list(sorted(L, key = len))
print("II Method- The longest string: ", s[len(s)-1])

def long_string(str1, L):
    s = list(sorted(L, key=len))
```

```
    print("III Function- The longest string: ", s[len(s) - 1])


long_string(str1, L)
```

9   nth index character from string

```
str1 = input("Enter a string: ")
index = int(input("Enter which index char required: "))
print("I & II Methods : The {} index char is:--> ".format(index), str1[index])
print("III Functions-->", end='')
def n_index(str1, index):
    for i in range(len(str1)):
        if i == index:
            print(str1[i])
            break


n_index(str1, index)
```

10   First last chars swapping

```
str1 = input("Enter a string: ")
L = list(str1)
L[0], L[len(str1)-1] = L[len(str1)-1], L[0]
new_str = "".join(L)
print("The given string is: ", str1)
print("I & II Methods The first & Last char swap is: ", new_str)

def first_last_swap(str1):
    L1 = list(str1)
    L1[0], L1[len(str1) - 1] = L1[len(str1) - 1], L1[0]
    print("III Function:", "".join(L1))
first_last_swap(str1)
```

11   Remove odd index values

```
str1 = input("Enter a string: ")
L = list(str1)
l = len(L)
print("The given string is: ", str1)
print("I & II Methods-The string removed with odd index: ", end='')
for i in range(l):
    if i % 2 == 0:
```

```python
        print(L[i], end='')

def remove_odd_Index(str1):
    L = list(str1)
    l = len(L)
    for i in range(l):
        if i % 2 == 0:
            print(L[i], end='')
print("\nIII Function-The string removed with odd index: ", end='')
remove_odd_Index(str1)
```

12   Count words in a string

```python
str1 = input("Enter a string: ")
l = str1.split(" ")
print(l)
print("I With BuitIn The NUmber of words: ", len(l))
count1 = 1
for char in str1:
    if char == ' ':
        count1 += 1
print("II Without buitIn The number of words:", count1)
def word_count(str1):
    count2 = 1
    for char1 in str1:
        if char1 == ' ':
            count2 += 1
    print("III Functions, The number of words:", count2)
word_count(str1)
```

13   Upper lower case of a string

```python
str1 = input("Enter a string: ")
print("I BuiltIn Upper case of given string: ", str1.upper())
print("I BuiltIn Lower case of given string: ", str1.lower())

def str_lower(str1):
    str_lower1 = ''
    for char1 in str1:
        if 65 <= ord(char1) <= 90:
            str_lower1 = str_lower1 + chr(ord(char1)+32)
```

```python
    else:
        str_lower1 = str_lower1 + char1
    print("II & III Function", str_lower1)
def str_upper(str1):
  str_upper1 = ''
  for char2 in str1:
    if 97 <= ord(char2) <= 122:
        str_upper1 = str_upper1 + chr(ord(char2)-32)
    else:
        str_upper1 = str_upper1 + char2
    print("II & III Function", str_upper1)
str_upper(str1)
str_lower(str1)
```

14   Sort unique words alphanumerically

```python
str1 = ['Bas', 'Apple', 'Cat', 'Zebra']
str2 = str1
# L_sort = sorted(set(L))
print("The given string is: ", str1)
print("I BuiltIn The sort of Unique alphanumeric string: ", sorted(str1))


L = []
l = len(str1)
for i in range(len(str2)):
   for j in range(i, l):
     if ord(str2[i][0]) < ord(str2[j][0]):
        if str1[i] not in L:
           L.append(str2[i])
     elif ord(str2[i][0]) > ord(str2[j][0]):
        if str1[j] not in L:
           L.append(str2[j])
else:
   L.append(str2[i])
print("II Without BuiltIn", L)
def sort_unique(str1):
   print("III Function, The sort of Unique alphanumeric string: ", sorted(str1))


sort_unique(str1)
```

15   Create html from string

```python
str1 = input("Enter the string: ")
tag1 = 'h1'
tag2 = 'b'
# x = 10
print("II Without BuiltIn:")
print("<%s>%s</%s>" % (tag1, str1, tag1))
print("<%s>%s</%s>" % (tag2, str1, tag2))
# print("<%i>" % x)
# print("<%f>" % x)
print("III Functions: ")
def HTML_tags(str1):
    tag1 = 'h1'
    tag2 = 'b'
    print("<%s>%s</%s>" % (tag1, str1, tag1))
    print("<%s>%s</%s>" % (tag2, str1, tag2))
HTML_tags(str1)
```

16   Insert string in middle of special chars

```python
str1 = input("Enter a string: ")
sub_str = input("Enter the substring: ")
L = list(str1)
position = len(str1)//2

L.insert(position, sub_str)
new_str = "".join(L)
print("I Built In Sub string at middle: ", new_str)

new_str1 = ''
new_str1 = str1[0:position]+sub_str+str1[position:]
print("II Without BuiltIn", new_str1)
def insert_mid(str1, position):
    new_str2 = ''
    new_str2 = str1[0:position] + sub_str + str1[position:]
    print("III Function", new_str2)

insert_mid(str1, position)
```

17   4 Copies of last 2 chars

```python
str1 = input("Enter a string: ")
pos_s, pos_e = int(input("Enter start position: ")), int(input("Enter end position: "))
cop_n = int(input("Enter number of copies: "))

if pos_s <= pos_e:
    # cop_n = int(input("Enter number of copies: "))
    str_new = str1[pos_s:pos_e+1] * cop_n
    print("II Without BuiltIN, The {} copies of string from {} to {} positions:".format(cop_n, pos_s, pos_e))
    print(str_new)
else:
    print("Please enter valid indexes")
def n_copies(str1, pos_s, pos_e, cop_n):
    if pos_s <= pos_e:
        # cop_n = int(input("Enter number of copies: "))
        str_new = str1[pos_s:pos_e + 1] * cop_n
        print("III Function, The {} copies of string from {} to {} positions:".format(cop_n, pos_s, pos_e))
        print(str_new)
    else:
        print("Please enter valid indexes")
n_copies(str1, pos_s, pos_e, cop_n)
```

18   Length of first 3 chars

```python
str1 = input("Enter a string: ")
print("I BuiltIn The length of first 3 chars: ", len(str1[0:3]))
count1 = 0
for i in str1[0:3]:
    count1 += 1
print("II Without BuiltIn", count1)


def len_string():
    print("III Function The length of first 3 chars: ", len(str1[0:3]))
len_string()
```

19   Last part of string

```python
str1 = "Hai This is DQ solutions working on IT"
L = str1.split()
print(L)
print("I Built In The last part of the string:->", L[-1])
```

```python
str_rev = str1[::-1]
wr = ''
for ch in str_rev:
    if ch != ' ':
        wr = ch + wr
    else:
        print("II Without BuiltIn-->", wr)
        break
def last_part(str1):
    L = str1.split()
    #print(L)
    print("III Function The last part of the string:->", L[-1])
last_part(str1)
```

20   reverses a string if it's length is a multiple of 4

```python
str1 = input("Enter a string: ")
if len(str1) % 4 == 0:
    print("I BuiltIn-The reverse of the string is: ", str1[::-1])
else:
    print("I BuiltIn The string length is not multiple of 4: ")


count1 = 0
for i in str1:
    count1 += 1
if count1 % 4 == 0:
    print("II without BuiltIn-The reverse of the string is:", str1[::-1])
else:
    print("II without BuiltIn The string length is not multiple of 4:")



def rev_mul4(str1):
    if len(str1) % 4 == 0:
        print("III Function-The reverse of the string is: ", str1[::-1])
    else:
        print("III Function The string length is not multiple of 4: ")
rev_mul4(str1)
```

21   Convert a given string to all uppercase

```python
str1 = input("Enter a string: ")
print("I BuiltIn Uppercase:", str1.upper())


str_upper2 = ''
for char1 in str1:
    if 97 <= ord(char1) <= 122:
        str_upper2 = str_upper2 + chr(ord(char1)-32)
    else:
        str_upper2 = str_upper2 + char1
print("II Without BuiltIn Uppercase:", str_upper2)



def str_upper(str1):
    str_upper1 = ''
    for char2 in str1:
        if 97 <= ord(char2) <= 122:
            str_upper1 = str_upper1 + chr(ord(char2)-32)
        else:
            str_upper1 = str_upper1 + char2
    print("III Function string Upper", str_upper1)


str_upper(str1)
```

22   program to sort a string lexicographically

```python
str1 = input("Enter a string:")
L = list(str1)
L1 = sorted(L, key = ord)  # ord return(int) unicode(ascii) of single character.
print("I BuiltIn The lexically ordered string:", "".join(L1))



length = len(str1)
for i in range(length):
    for j in range(i+1, length):
        if ord(L[i]) > ord(L[j]):
            L[i], L[j] = L[j], L[i]


print("II without BuiltIn:", "".join(L))


def sort_lexically(str1, L):
    L1 = sorted(L, key=ord)  # ord return(int) unicode(ascii) of single character.
```

```python
    print("III Functions:", "".join(L1))
sort_lexically(str1, L)
```

23   program to remove a newline in Python

```python
str1 = "V Solutions\n is \n giving IT Training"
L = list(str1)
new_str = " "

for i in L:
    if i == '\n':
        continue
    else:
        new_str += i
print("I & II without BuiltIn new line removal:", new_str)

def remove_nline(str1):
    L1 = []
    L1 = str1.split('\n')
    print("III Function new line removal:", "".join(L1))
remove_nline(str1)
```

24   program to check whether a string starts with specified characters

```python
str1 = input("Enter the string: ")
sub_str = input("Enter substring to check at start: ")
l = len(sub_str)
if str1[0:l] == sub_str:
    print("I & II without BuiltIn YES..The string started with given sub_string:{}".format(sub_str))
else:
    print("I & II without BuiltIn NO..The string was not started with given string:{}".format(sub_str))

def start_with_char(str1, sub_str):
    if str1[0:l] == sub_str:
        print("III Function, YES..The string started with given sub_string:{}".format(sub_str))
    else:
        print("III Function, NO..The string was not started with given string:{}".format(sub_str))

start_with_char(str1, sub_str)
```

25   program to create a Caesar encryption

```python
str1 = input("Enter a string: ")
ce_shift = int(input("Enter encode shift positions: "))
enc_str = ''
for i in str1:
    if i.isupper():
        char = chr(((ord(i) - 65) + ce_shift) % 26 + 65)
        enc_str += char
    elif i.islower():
        char = chr(((ord(i) - 97) + ce_shift) % 26 + 97)
        enc_str += char
    else:
        print("Please enter valid string: ")


print("I & II without BuiltIn The encoded string is: ", enc_str)
def ceaser_enc(str1, ce_shift):
    enc_str = ''
    for i in str1:
        if i.isupper():
            char = chr(((ord(i) - 65) + ce_shift) % 26 + 65)
            enc_str += char
        elif i.islower():
            char = chr(((ord(i) - 97) + ce_shift) % 26 + 97)
            enc_str += char
        else:
            print("Please enter valid string: ")
    print("III Function, The encoded string is: ", enc_str)
ceaser_enc(str1, ce_shift)
```

26   display formatted text (width=50) as output

```python
str1 = "Python was created by Guido van Rossum during 1985- 1990. Python is a general-purpose
interpreted, \
interactive, object-oriented, and high-level programming language. "
import textwrap
new_str = textwrap.fill(str1, width=20)
print("\nI with BuiltIn\n", new_str)


print(" \nII without BuiltIn\n")
count1 = 0
for ch in str1:
```

```python
    if count1 != 20:
        print(ch, end='')
        count1 += 1
    elif count1 == 20:
        print(ch, end='')
        count1 = 0
        print()

def test_wrap(str1):
    new_str1 = textwrap.fill(str1, width=20)
    print("\nIII Function\n", new_str1)
test_wrap(str1)
```

27   remove existing indentation from all of the lines in a given text

```python
str1 = '''
    Hai This is the world
    with people having technical
    skills '''
print(str1)
import textwrap
print("\nI with BuiltIn\n", textwrap.dedent(str1))

print("\nII without BuiltIn\n")
word = ''
L_word = []
index = 0
for ch in str1:
    if ch != '\n':
        word = word + ch
    else:
        L_word.append(word)
        word = ''
else:
    L_word.append(word)
for word in L_word:
    print(word[7:])

def Indent_del(str1):
    print("\nIII Function-- Indent remove\n", textwrap.dedent(str1))
```

```
Indent_del(str1)
```

28   to add a prefix text to all of the lines in a string

```python
import textwrap
str1 = '''
Hai we are not great people
like gandhi, nehru
but some people are great.
'''
print("I with BuiltIn", textwrap.indent(str1, ">>>"))
print("II without BuiltIn")
word = ''
L_word = []
for ch in str1:
    if ch != '\n':
        word = word + ch
    else:
        L_word.append(word)
        word = ''
else:
    L_word.append(word)
for word in L_word:
    if word != '':
        print('>>>', word)
def indent_(str1):
    print("III Function\n", textwrap.indent(str1, ">>>"))
indent_(str1)
```

29   to set the indentation of the first line

```python
str1 = '''
Hai many people are
thinking that they
Know everything but
we are nothing
'''
import textwrap
print("I With BuiltIn\n", textwrap.fill(str1, initial_indent='^^^', width=20))
```

```python
print("\nII Without BuiltIn\n")
word = ''
L_word = []
for ch in str1:
    if ch != '\n':
        word = word + ch
    else:
        L_word.append(word)
        word = ''
else:
    L_word.append(word)
print(">>>", end='')
for word in L_word:
    if word != '':
        print(word)
def first_indent(str1):
    print("III Function\n", textwrap.fill(str1, initial_indent='^^^', width=20))
first_indent(str1)
```

30   to print the following floating numbers upto 2 decimal places

```python
num1 = 20.3456
num2 = 13.67893
print("I with builtIns")
print("The num1 with 2 decimal points: {:.2f}".format(num1))
print("The num2 with 3 decimal points: {:.3f}".format(num2))
word = ''
L_word = []
for i in str(num1):
    if i != '.':
        word = word+i
    else:
        L_word.append(word)
        L_word.append('.')
        word = ''
else:
    L_word.append(word)
L_word[2] = L_word[2][1:3]
print("\nII without builtIn", "".join(L_word))

def float_formats(num1, num2):
```

```python
    print("The num1 with 2 decimal points: {:.2f}".format(num1))
    print("The num2 with 3 decimal points: {:.3f}".format(num2))
print("\nIII Function\n")
float_formats(num1, num2)
```

31   print the following floating numbers upto 2 decimal places with a sign

```python
num1 = float(input("Enter number:"))
print("Two decimal points: {:.2f}".format(num1))
print("I BuiltIn {} rounded value is :".format(num1), round(num1))


def float_signed(num1):
    print("Two decimal points: {:.2f}".format(num1))
    print("III Functions, {} rounded value is :".format(num1), round(num1))


float_signed(num1)
```

32   print the following floating numbers with no decimal places

```python
num1 = float(input("Enter a number: "))
print("I with or without BuiltIn")
print("The number is with no decimal: {:.0f}".format(num1))
print("The number is with no decimal: %.0f" % num1)
print("The number is with no decimal:", round(num1))


def float_no_decimal(num1):
    print("I. The number is with no decimal: {:.0f}".format(num1))
    print("II. The number is with no decimal: %.0f" % num1)
    print("III. The number is with no decimal:", round(num1))
print("III Functions")
float_no_decimal(num1)
```

33   print the following integers with zeros on the left of specified width

```python
# {:0>6d} - if the symbol is '>', * is padded on left to make its width 6
# {:0<7d} - if the symbol is '<', * is padded on right to make its width 7

num = int(input("Enter a number: "))
print("\n I BuiltIn Method \n")
print("The number pre padded with zeros:", str(num).rjust(6,'0'))
print("The number post padded with *s:",str(num).ljust(6,'*'))
print("\n II without BuiltIn\n")
```

```python
print("The number pre padded with zeros: {:0>6d}".format(num))
print("The number post padded with *s:  {:*<6d}".format(num))
def fun_pading(num):
    print("\n III Functions\n")
    print("The number pre padded with zeros:",str(num).rjust(6, '0'))
    print("The number post padded with *s:",str(num).ljust(6, '*'))
fun_pading(num)
```

34   print the following integers with '*' on the right of specified width

35   to display a number with a comma separator

```python
num1 = int(input("Enter a number"))
print("II without BuiltIn,The comma seperator value is: {:,}".format(num1))

def comma_sep(num1):
    print("III Functions, The comma seperator value is: {:,}".format(num1))
comma_sep(num1)
```

36   to format a number with a percentage

```python
num = int(input("Enter a number: "))
print("II without BuiltIn, The formatted number with is %d" % num)
def format(num):
    print("III Function, The formatted number with is %d" % num)
format(num)
```

37   to display a number in left, right and center aligned of width 10

```python
num = int(input("Enter a number: "))
print("The left aligned number: {:*>10d}".format(num))
print("The right aligned number: {:*<10d}".format(num))
s = "Hello"
print(s.center(10, "*"))
```

38   to count occurrences of a substring in a string

```python
str1 = input("Enter a string: ")
sub_str = input("Enter sub string:")
print("The occurrence of sub string--" + sub_str + "--is:", str1.count(sub_str))
print("Reverse of the given string is: ", str1[::-1])

def rev(str1):
```

```python
    estr = ''
    for c in str1:
        estr = c + estr
    print("III Function ", estr)
rev(str1)
```

39   reverse a string

```python
str1 = input("Enter a string: ")
sub_str = input("Enter sub string:")
print("The occurrence of sub string--" + sub_str + "--is:", str1.count(sub_str))
print("Reverse of the given string is: ", str1[::-1])

def rev(str1):
    estr = ''
    for c in str1:
        estr = c + estr
    print("III Function ", estr)
rev(str1)
```

40   reverse words in a string

```python
str1 = input("Enter a string: ")
L = str1.split()
print("I & II without built In-->", end=' ')
for i in L:
    print(i[::-1], end=' ')

print("\nIII Functions-->", end=' ')
def rev(str1):
    estr = ''
    for c in str1:
        estr = c + estr
    return estr
def rev_words(L):
    for word in L:
        print(rev(word), end=' ')
rev_words(L)
```

41   strip a set of characters from a string

```python
str1 = "IT solutions in bangalore"
sub_str = 'bangalore'
print("I BuiltIn-->", str1.strip(sub_str))
L = []
for word in str1.split():
    if word != sub_str:
        L.append(word)
print("II without Builtin-->", " ".join(L))


def sub_str_strip(str1, sub_str):
    L1 = []
    for word in str1.split():
        if word != sub_str:
            L1.append(word)
    print("III Functions-->", " ".join(L1))
sub_str_strip(str1, sub_str)
```

42   count repeated characters in a string

```python
str1 = "V solutions"
L = []
for i in str1:
    if str1.count(i) > 1:
        L.append(i)
print("I with BuiltIn", list(set(L)))


dict1 ={}

for i in range(len(str1)):
    count = 1
    for j in range(i + 1, len(str1)):
        if str1[i] == str1[j]:
            count += 1
            dict1[str1[i]] = count
print("II without BuiltIn, The repeated chars", dict1.keys())


def rep_chars(str1):
    L1 = []
    for i in str1:
        if str1.count(i) > 1:
            L1.append(i)
```

```python
    print("III Functions", list(set(L1)))

rep_chars(str1)
```

43   square and cube symbol in the area of a rectangle and volume of a cylinder

```python
radius = float(input("Enter area:"))
pi = 3.14
area = pi * radius * radius
vol = 4/3 * pi * radius * radius * radius
print("I & II without builtIn, The area is: {:.2f} and volume is: {:.2f}".format(area, vol))


def area_rad(radius):
    pi = 3.14
    area = pi * radius * radius
    vol = 4 / 3 * pi * radius * radius * radius
    print("III Function, The area is: {:.2f} and volume is: {:.2f}".format(area, vol))


area_rad(radius)
```

44   print the index of the character in a string

```python
str1 = input("Enter a string: ")
ch = input("Enter a char to find index:")
print("I BuiltIn, The index of given char is: ", str1.index(ch))

for c in range(len(str1)):
    if str1[c] == ch:
        print("II without BuiltIn The index of given char is", c)
        break
else:
    print("char not available")

def find_index(str1):
    for c in range(len(str1)):
        if str1[c] == ch:
            print("III Function- The index of given char is", c)
            break
        else:
            print("char not available")
find_index(str1)
```

45   check if a string contains all letters of the alphabet

```
str1 = input("Enter a string: ")
L = list(str1)
S = list(set(L))
print(S)
c = 0
L = []
for i in S:
   if i.isalpha():
      c += 1
if c == 26:
   print("I & II without BuiltIn, All Alphabets PRESENT in given string:")
else:
   print("I & II without BuiltIn, All Alphabets NOT PRESENT: ")


def chk_all_alphabet(str1):
   c1 = 0
   for i1 in S:
      if i1.isalpha():
         c1 += 1
   if c1 == 26:
      print("III Functions, All Alphabets PRESENT in given string:")
   else:
      print("III Functions, All Alphabets NOT PRESENT: ")


chk_all_alphabet(str1)
```

46   convert a string in a list

```
str1 = input("Enter a string: ")
L = list(str1)
S = list(set(L))
print(S)
c = 0
L = []
for i in S:
   if i.isalpha():
      c += 1
if c == 26:
   print("I & II without BuiltIn, All Alphabets PRESENT in given string:")
```

```python
else:
    print("I & II without BuiltIn, All Alphabets NOT PRESENT: ")

def chk_all_alphabet(str1):
    c1 = 0
    for i1 in S:
        if i1.isalpha():
            c1 += 1
    if c1 == 26:
        print("III Functions, All Alphabets PRESENT in given string:")
    else:
        print("III Functions, All Alphabets NOT PRESENT: ")


chk_all_alphabet(str1)
```

47   lowercase first n characters in a string

```python
str1 = input("Enter a string: ")
n = int(input("Enter how chars you want:"))
c = 0
for i in str1:
    if i.islower():
        print(i, end=' ')
        c += 1
        if c == n:
            break
        else:
            continue
```

48   swap comma and dot in a string

```python
str1 = input("Enter a string: ")
L = list(str1)
for i in range(len(L)):
    if L[i] == ',':
        c = i
    elif L[i] == '.':
        d = i
    else:
        continue
```

```python
L[c], L[d] = L[d], L[c]
print("After swap comma and dot: ", ''.join(L))
```

49   count and display the vowels of a given text

```python
str1 = input("Enter a string: ")
v_list = ['a', 'e', 'i', 'o', 'u']
c = 0
for i in str1:
    if i.lower() in v_list:
        c += 1
print("The count of vowels in the string are: ", c)
```

50   split a string on the last occurrence of the delimiter

```python
str1 = input("Enter a string: ")
print(str1.rsplit(',', 1))
```

51   find the first non-repeating character in given string

```python
str1 = input("Enter a string: ")
L = list(str1)
for i in L:
    if L.count(i) == 1:
        print('The first non repeating char is:', i)
        break
```

52   print all permutations with given repetition number of given string

```python
str1 = input("Enter a string: ")
p_no = int(input("Enter p_no: "))
for i in range(1, p_no+1):
    print(str1 * i)
```

53   find the first repeated character in a given string

```python
str1 = input("Enter a string: ")
L = list(str1)
for i in L:
    if L.count(i) > 1:
        print('The first non repeating char is:', i)
        break
```

54   find the first repeated character of a given string where the index of first occurrence is smallest

```
str1 = input("Enter a string: ")
L = list(str1)
for i in L:
    if L.count(i) > 1:
        print('The first non repeating char is:', i)
        break
```

55   find the first repeated word in a given string

```
str1 = input("Enter a string: ")
L = str1.split()
for i in L:
    if L.count(i) > 1:
        print("The first repeated word:", i)
        break
```

56   find the second most repeated word in a given string

```
str1 = input("Enter a string: ")
L = str1.split()
c = 0
for i in L:
    if L.count(i) > 1:
        c += 1
        if c == 2:
            print("The second most repeated word:", i)
            break

else:
    print("No such repeated words")
```

57   remove spaces from a given string

```
str1 = input("Enter a string: ")
L = str1.split()
print("The space removed string", "".join(L))
```

58   move spaces to the front of a given string

```python
import textwrap
str1 = input("Enter a string: ")
c = str1.count(' ')
spaces = ' ' * c
L = str1.split()
print(L)
new_str = "".join(L)
print(textwrap.fill(new_str, initial_indent=spaces))
```

59   find the maximum occurring character in a given string

```python
str1 = input("Enter a string: ")
length = len(str1)
L = list(str1)
for i in range(length):
    for j in range(i+1, length):
        if L.count(L[i]) < L.count(L[j]):
            max_char = j
        else:
            max_char = i

print("The character with high frequency is: ", L[max_char])
```

60   capitalize first and last letters of each word of a given string

```python
str1 = input("Enter a string: ")
title_str1 = str1.title()
L = title_str1.split()
new_word = ''
new_str = ''
for word in L:
    new_word = word[0:len(word)-1] + word[-1].upper()
    new_str = new_str + " " + new_word
print('The converted string: ', new_str)
```

61   remove duplicate characters of a given string

```python
str1 = input("Enter a string: ")
L = list(str1)
L1 = L.copy()
```

```python
length_L = len(L1)
for i in range(0, length_L):
   if L1.count(L1[i]) > 1:
      L.remove(L1[i])
print(L)
```

62   compute sum of digits of a given string

```python
str1 = input("Enter a string: ")
sum1 = 0
for char in str1:
   if char.isdigit():
      sum1 = sum1 + int(char)
print("The sum of digits: ", sum1)
```

63   remove leading zeros from an IP address

```python
str1 = input("Enter a string: ")
L = str1.split(':')
new_list = []
for word in L:
   new_list.append(word.lstrip('0'))
print(":".join(new_list))
```

64   Reverse a given string Input : "Python"   Output : "nohtyP"

```python
str1 = input("Enter a string: ")
L = str1.split()
new_str = ''
for word in L:
   new_str = new_str + ' ' + word[::-1]
print("The reversed words:", new_str)
```

65   Reverse each word in given string Input

```python
str1 = input("Enter a string: ")
L = str1.split()
new_str = ''
for word in L:
   new_str = new_str + ' ' + word[::-1]
print("The reversed words:", new_str)
```

66   Reverse each word and reverse word again. Input

```
str1 = input("Enter a string: ")
new_str1 = ''
new_str2 = ''
word_r1 = ''
word_r2 = ''
L = str1.split()
for word in L:
    word_r1 = word[::-1]
    word_r2 = word_r1[::-1]
    new_str1 = new_str1 + " " + word_r1
    new_str2 = new_str2 + " " + word_r2
print("The single reverse: ", new_str1)
print("The double reverse: ", new_str2)
```

67   that accepts a string and calculate the number of digits and letters

```
str1 = input("Enter a string: ")
d = a = 0
for char in str1:
    if char.isdigit():
        d = d + 1
    elif char.isalpha():
        a = a + 1
    else:
        continue
print("The count of digits:", d)
print("The count of alphabets:", a)
```

LIST

1   Sum of elements

```
L = [1, 2, 3, 4]
print("The sum of elements of List is:", sum(L))
m = 1
for i in L:
    m = m * i
print("The multiplied value of:", m)
```

2   Mulitply of elements

```python
L = [1, 2, 3, 4]
print("The sum of elements of List is:", sum(L))
m = 1
for i in L:
    m = m * i
print("The multiplied value of:", m)
```

3   Largest number from list

```python
L = [12, 33, 56, 100]
print("The max element: ", max(L))
print("the min element: ", min(L))
```

4   Smallest number from list

```python
L = [12, 33, 56, 100]
print("The max element: ", max(L))
print("the min element: ", min(L))
```

5   Count no of strings whose length is 2

```python
str1 = input("Enter a string: ")
L = str1.split()
c = 0
for word in L:
    if len(word) == 2:
        print(word)
        c += 1
print("The number words with length 2 are: ", c)
```

6   Sort elements in increasing order

```python
L = [23, 44, 1, 56, 11, 34]
L.sort()
print("The ascending order:", L)
L.sort(reverse=True)
print("The descending order:", L)
```

7   Remove duplicates

```python
L = [1, 2, 3, 5, 1, 2, 5]
print("After removal of duplicates:", list(set(L)))
```

8   Check list is empty or not

```
L = []
ln = int(input("Enter length of List:"))
for i in range(ln):
   ele = input("Enter element: ")
   L.append(ele)
if len(L) == 0:
   print("The list is EMPTY:")
else:
   print("The list is NOT EMPTY:")
```

9   Clone or copy

```
L = []
ln = int(input("Enter length of List:"))
for i in range(ln):
   print("Enter {} element: ".format(i+1), end='')
   ele = input()
   L.append(ele)
new_list = L.copy()
print("The given list:", L)
print("The new copy of the list:", new_list)
```

10   Words that are longer than any element

```
str1 = input("Enter a string: ")
L = str1.split()
Ln_List = []
for word in L:
   Ln_List.append(len(word))
for word in L:
   If len(word) == max(Ln_LIst):
      print("The longest word in given string is:", word)
      break
```

11   Find common element from 2 lists

```
L1 = []
L2 = []
ln = int(input("Enter length of first List:"))
for i in range(ln):
```

```python
    print("Enter {} element: ".format(i+1), end='')
    ele = input()
    L1.append(ele)

ln = int(input("Enter length of second List:"))
for i in range(ln):
    print("Enter {} element: ".format(i+1), end='')
    ele = input()
    L2.append(ele)

C = [ele for ele in L1 if ele in L2]
print(C)
```

12 Remove specified index from list and print

```python
L1 = []
ln = int(input("Enter length of List:"))
for i in range(ln):
    print("Enter {} index element: ".format(i), end='')
    ele = input()
    L1.append(ele)

ind = int(input("Enter index of element to be removed:"))
print("Before removal of index element:", L1)
L1.pop(ind)
print("After removal of index element:", L1)
```

13 Write 3D array

```python
L = [[[2, 3, 4], [1, 2, 3], [4, 5, 6]]]
print("The 0th indexed row and 0th index column list:", L[0][0])
print("The 0th indexed row and 1th index column list:", L[0][1])
print("The 0th indexed row and 2nd index column list:", L[0][2])
print("The 0th indexed row and 1th index column 1st index element:", L[0][1][1])
```

14 Remove even elements and print list

```python
L1 = []
ln = int(input("Enter length of List:"))
for i in range(ln):
    print("Enter {} element: ".format(i+1), end='')
    ele = int(input())
```

```
L1.append(ele)
print(" The even numbers list is: ", [x for x in L1 if x % 2 != 0])
```

15   Shuffle list and print

```
import random
L = [1, 2, 3, 4, 10, 22, 14]
random.shuffle(L)
print("The shuffled list is: ", L)
```

16   First, Last elements whose square value is between 1 and 30

```
L1 = []
ln = int(input("Enter length of List:"))
for i in range(ln):
    print("Enter {} element: ".format(i+1), end='')
    ele = int(input())
    L1.append(ele)
first = L1[0] * L1[0]
last = L1[ln-1] * L1[ln-1]
if 1 <= first < 30:
    print("The square of first element:", first)
if 1 <= last < 30:
    print("The square of last element:", last)
else:
    print("{}, {} elements squares in 1 to 30:".format(L1[0], L1[ln-1]))
```

17   First, Last elements whose square value is between 1 and 30,except first 5

18   All permutations of list elements

```
import itertools
L1 = []
ln = int(input("Enter length of List:"))
for i in range(ln):
    print("Enter {} element: ".format(i+1), end='')
    ele = input()
    L1.append(ele)
```

```python
P = list(itertools.permutations(L1))
print(P)
```

19   Difference between 2 lists

```python
L1 = [2, 3, 4, 5, 6]
L2 = [5, 6, 7, 4, 2]
D = [x for x in L1 if x not in L2]
print(D)
```

20   To access index of list

```python
L1 = [2, 4, 66, 7, 9]
ele = int(input("Enter element to access index: "))
if ele in L1:
    print("The index is:",  L1.index(ele))
else:
    print("Enter a valid element..")
```

21   List of characters into string

```python
L1 = []
ln = int(input("Enter length of List:"))
for i in range(ln):
    print("Enter {} element: ".format(i+1), end='')
    ele = input()
    L1.append(ele)
print("The given list is:", L1)
print("The string from the list:", " ".join(L1))
```

22   Finding index of an item in specified list

```python
L1 = [2, 4, 66, 7, 9]
ele = int(input("Enter element to access index: "))
if ele in L1:
    print("The index is:",  L1.index(ele))
else:
    print("Enter a valid element..")
```

23   Flatten a shallow

```
import itertools
L1 = [[2, 4, 5, 6, 7], [34, 22, 12, 0]]
L2 = L1.copy()
F = list(itertools.chain.from_iterable(L1))
print("The flatten list is: ", F)
```

24   Append a list to second list

```
L1 = [1, 2, 4, 55, 65]
L2 = [23, 24, 22, 12]
print("The given list are:", L1, L2)
L1.append(L2)
print("The second list appended to first list:", L1)
```

25   Select an item randomly

```
import random
L1 = [22, 4, 6, 12, 27, 90, 3]
print("The random selection from List is:", random.choice(L1))
```

26   Check circularly identical in two lists

```
L1 = [10, 10, 0, 0, 10]
L2 = [10, 10, 10, 0, 0]  # identical
# L2 = [1, 10, 10, 0, 0] # Not Identical
L1.extend(L1)

for i in range(len(L1)):
    if L2 == L1[i:i+len(L2)]:
        print(" L1 and L2 are Circularly Identical:")
        break
else:
    print("L1 and L2 are Not Circularly Identical:")
```

27   Finding a second smallest number

```
L1 = [12, 22, 34, 55, 46, 21]
L1.sort()
print("The sorted list is:", L1)
print("The second smallest is: ", L1[1])
print("The second largest is: ", L1[-2])
```

28 Finding a second largest number

```
L1 = [12, 22, 34, 55, 46, 21]
L1.sort()
print("The sorted list is:", L1)
print("The second smallest is: ", L1[1])
print("The second largest is: ", L1[-2])
```

29 Get unique values

```
L1 = [12, 12, 34, 5, 5, 66, 77, 77, 87]
print("The unique values in list are list:", list(set(L1)))
```

30 Frequency of elements

```
import collections
# from collections import Counter
L1 = [12, 12, 34, 5, 5, 66, 77, 77, 87]
print("The frequency of elements:", collections.Counter(L1))
```

31 Counting number elements within a specified ranges

```
L1 = [12, 10, 11, 13, 25, 36, 41]
S = int(input("Enter start of range:"))
E = int(input("Enter end of range:"))
c = 0
for ele in L1:
    if S <= ele <= E:
        print(ele)
        c += 1
if c == 0:
    print("No elements in range {} {}".format(S, E))
else:
    print("A total of {} elements present in range ({}, {})".format(c, S, E))
```

32 Check a list contains sub list

```
L1 = [10, 22, 3, 45, [2, 3, 4], 6]
L2 = [2, 5, 6, 77, 9]
for i in L1:
    if type(i) == list:
        print("Sublist present in the given list.")
        break
```

```
else:
    print("No sublist present in given list.")
```

33   Generate all sub lists

```
L1 = [10, 22, 3, 45]
SL = []
B = [[]]
for i in range(len(L1)+1):
    for j in range(i+1, len(L1)+1):
        SL = L1[i:j]
        B.append(SL)
print("II without BuiltIn functions:", B)
def sublist_gen(L1):
    SL1 = []
    B1 = [[]]
    for i in range(len(L1) + 1):
        for j in range(i + 1, len(L1) + 1):
            SL1 = L1[i:j]
            B1.append(SL1)
    print("III Functions:", B1)
sublist_gen(L1)
```

34   Printing elements in ascending order

```
L1 = [12, 1, 2, 3, 55, 67, 89, 100, 3]
L1.sort()
print("The ascending order of elements: ", L1)
```

35   Create a list by concatenating a given list which range goes from 1 to n

```
L1 = [2, 3, 5, 7, 9]
L2 = [100]
L3 = L1 + L2
print("The concatenation on list:", L3)
```

36   Variable unique identification number

```
L = ["hai", "hello", "kilo"]
for ele in L:
    if ele.isidentifier():
```

```
        print(ele)
    else:
        pass
```

37   Finding common items from two lists

```
L1 = [1, 2, 3, 4, 55]
L2 = [22, 2, 3, 4, 10]
Common = [ele for ele in L1 if ele in L2]
print("The common elements in the two lists are:", Common)
```

38   Change the position of every nth value with (n+1)th value

```
L = [11, 22, 33, 44, 55]
p = int(input("Enter nth position to change:"))
if -1 < p < len(L):
    print("The initial list:", L)
    L[p], L[p+1] = L[p+1], L[p]
    print("The updated list:", L)
else:
    print("Enter a valid index position.")
```

39   Converting multiple integers into single integer

```
L = [1, 2, 3, 4, 5, 6]
L_str = ''
for ele in L:
    L_str = L_str + (str(ele))

print("The converted list:", int(L_str))
```

40   Split a list based on first character of word

```
str1 = "hai hello please help honestly"
L = str1.split(str1[0])
print(L)
```


41   Create multiple list

```
# Create a list
L1 = []
length = int(input("Enter size: "))
```

```
for i in range(length):
    ele = int(input("Enter {} element:".format(i+1)))
    L1.append(ele)
print("The given list is:", L1)


# Find missing value in given range
SN = int(input("Enter start of range:"))
EN = int(input("Enter end of range:"))
range_list = [x for x in range(SN, EN+1)]
missed_list = [ele for ele in L1 if ele not in range_list]
print("The missed element in given range:", missed_list)
```

42   Find missing and additional values

```
# Create a list
L1 = []
length = int(input("Enter size: "))
for i in range(length):
    ele = int(input("Enter {} element:".format(i+1)))
    L1.append(ele)
print("The given list is:", L1)


# Find missing value in given range
SN = int(input("Enter start of range:"))
EN = int(input("Enter end of range:"))
range_list = [x for x in range(SN, EN+1)]
missed_list = [ele for ele in L1 if ele not in range_list]
print("The missed element in given range:", missed_list)
```

43   Split a list into different variables

```
import random

L1 = [int(random.random()*100) for i in range(10)]
L_var1 = L1[0:3]
L_var2 = L1[3:10]
print("The generated list is:", L1)
print("The first variable:", L_var1)
print("The second variable:", L_var2)
```

44   Generate group of five consecutive numbers in a list

```
start = int(input("Enter starting number:"))
L1 = [x for x in range(start, start + 5)]
print(L1)
```

45   Convert a pair of values into a sorted unique array

```
L1 = [10, 23, 25, 37, 29, 30]
length = len(L1)
print(L1)


for i in range(length):
   for j in range(i+1, length):
      if L1[i] > L1[j]:
         L1[i], L1[j] = L1[j], L1[i]
print("The consecutive sort:", L1)
```

46   Slect odd items of a list

```
import random

L1 = [random.randint(10, 100) for x in range(1, 11)]
print("The generated list is: ", L1)
print(list(ele for ele in L1 if ele % 2 == 1))
```

47   Insert an element before each element of a list

```
import random
L1 = [random.randint(10, 100) for x in range(1, 6)]
L2 = []
print("The given list is:", L1)
for i in range(0, 2*len(L1), 2):
   ele = int(input("Enter element to insert before index {} :".format(i)))
   L1.insert(i, ele)
   print("The list after insertion:", L1)
```

48   Print a nested lists (each list on a new line) using the print() function

```
L1 = [10, 20, 30, [1, 2, 3, 5], [10, 11, 13], 55, 70]
for ele in L1:
   if type(ele) != list:
      print(ele, end=' ')
   else:
```

```
    print()
    print(ele)
```

49   Convert list to list of dictionaries

```
import random

L_keys = ["Apple", 'Banana', "Cherry", "Dragon"]
D = {}
for i, j in enumerate(L_keys, random.randint(10, 100)):
    D[j] = i
print(D)


for i, j in enumerate(L_keys, 10):
    D[j] = i
print(D)
```

50   Sort a list of nested dictionaries

```
import random
L_keys = ['Banana', "Apple", "Dragon", "Cherry"]
D = {}
for i, j in enumerate(L_keys, random.randint(10, 100)):
    D[j] = i

print("The given list is:", D)
L_sort = list(D)
L_sort.sort()
print("The sorted list is:", L_sort)
```

51   Split a list every Nth element

```
L1 = [10, 20, 30, 33, 44, 56, 71]
num = int(input("Enter a number for split:"))
Ind = L1.index(num)
C1 = 0
L2 = [ele for ele in L1[0:Ind]]
L3 = [ele for ele in L1[Ind:len(L1)]]
print(L2)
print(L3)
```

52   Compute the similarity between two lists

```
L1 = [1, 2, 3, 4, 5]
L2 = [1, 2, 3, 4, 9]
if L1 == L2:
   print("EQUAL")
else:
   print(" NOT EQUAL")


print('L1 & L2 are EQUAL--->', L1 == L2)
print('L1 LESSER--->', L1 < L2)
print('L1 GREATER--->', L1 > L2)
```

53   Create a list with infinite elements

```
L1 = []
a = 0
while True:
   a += 1
   L1.append(a)
   print(L1)
```

54   Concatenate elements of a list

```
L1 = [1, 2, 3, 41, 5]
str1 = ''
for ele in L1:
   str1 = str1 + str(ele)
print(int(str1))
```

55   Remove key values pairs from a list of dictionaries

```
L1 = [{"Hanuman": 2, "kumar": 3, "vudata": 4}, {"hai": 11, "Kish": 12}]
print(L1)
print(L1[0])
print(L1[0].popitem())
print(L1)
```

56   Convert a string to a list

```
str1 = 'Hello boys please come'
L = list(str1)
print(L)
```

57   Check if all items of a list is equal to a given string

```python
str1 = 'Hello boys please come'
L = list(str1)
print(L)
```

58   Replace the last element in a list with another list

```python
L1 = [1, 2, 33, 4, 5]
L2 = [11, 22, 33, 44]
L1[-1] = L2
print("After replacing last element with list:", L1)
```

59   Check if the n-th element exists in a given list

```python
L1 = [10, 12, 13, 22, 34, 17]
n = int(input("Enter nth index: "))
if n > len(L1)-1:
    print("Element Not Exist:")
else:
    print("Element at index {} exists:".format(n), L1[n])
```

60   Find a tuple, the smallest second index value from a list of tuples

```python
L1 = [(1, 2, 3), (11, 2, 3), (10, 1, 15, 19)]
for tup in L1:
    if tup[1] == min(tup):
        print("The tuple with smallest 2nd element", tup)
```

61   Create a list of empty dictionaries

```python
L1 = [{}, {}, {}]
print(len(L1))
```

62   Print a list of space-separated elements

```python
str1 = "Hello the name is small"
L = str1.split()
print(L)
sub_str = input("Enter sub string:")
L.insert(0, sub_str)
print(L)
```

63   Insert a given string at the beginning of all items in a list

```
str1 = "Hello the name is small"
L = str1.split()
print(L)
sub_str = input("Enter sub string:")
L.insert(0, sub_str)
print(L)
```

64   Iterate over two lists simultaneously

```
L1 = [1, 2, 3, 44, 5, 67]
L2 = [11, 23, 4, 5, 67, 55]
for ele_L1, ele_L2 in zip(L1, L2):
    print(ele_L1, ele_L2)
```

65   Access dictionary keys element by index

```
D = {"hanuman": 1, "kumar": 2, "vudata": 3}

L1 = [ele for ele in D.keys()]
print(L1)
```

66   Find the list in a list of lists whose sum of elements is the highest

```
L1 = [[1, 2, 3], [10, 23], [10, 20, 40], [12, 100]]
SL_sum = []
for sublist in L1:
    SL_sum.append(sum(sublist))
for sublist in L1:
    if sum(sublist) == max(SL_sum):
        print(sublist)
```

67   Find all the values in a list are greater than a specified number

```
import random

L1 = [random.randint(10, 100) for i in range(1, 11)]
print("the given list:", L1)
num = int(input("Enter a number to get greater values:"))
for ele in L1:
    if ele > num:
        print(ele)
```

68   Extend a list without append

```
L1 = [1, 2, 3, 5, 11]
L2 = [11, 23, 24]
L1.extend(L2)
print(L1)
```

69   Remove duplicates from a list of lists

```
L1 = [[1, 1, 2, 3], [1, 2, 2, 3], [1, 1, 2], [1, 4, 7]]
L2 = []
for sublist in L1:
   L2. append(list(set(sublist)))
print("The given list is:", L1)
print("After removal of duplicates from list of lists:", L2)
```

70   Get the depth of a dictionary

```
D = {"han": 1, "kum":33, 'Vudata': {'hh': 20}}
str_dict = str(D)
print(str_dict)
c = 0
for i in str_dict:
   if i =='{':
      c += 1
print("The depth:", c)
```

71   Check if all dictionaries in a list are empty or not

```
L = [{}, {'h': 1}, [1, 2, 3]]

for i in L:
   if type(i) == dict and len(i) != 0:
      print("The dict is not empty:")
      break
else:
   print("empty dicts:")
```

72   Two digits m (row) and n (column) as input and generates a two-dimensional array. The element value in the i-th row and j-th column of the array should be i*j

```python
L = []
rows = int(input("Enter no of rows:"))
cols = int(input("Enter no of cols"))
for i in range(rows):
    for j in range(cols):
        print(i, j)

    print()
print(L)


L1 = [[i * j for i in range(cols)] for j in range(rows)]
print(L1)
```

73   A list contains group of strings. Convert each word to capital letter and print

```python
str1 = "hello hai please come"
L = str1.split()
L_upper = [word.upper() for word in L]
print(L_upper)
L_reverse = [word[::-1] for word in L_upper]
print(L_reverse)
```

74   Reverse list of elements and print in upper case

```python
str1 = "hello hai please come"
L = str1.split()
L_upper = [word.upper() for word in L]
print(L_upper)
L_reverse = [word[::-1] for word in L_upper]
print(L_reverse)
```

75   Write a Python program to convert month name to a number of days

```python
month_to_days = {
    "January": 31,
    "February": 28,  # Assuming a non-leap year
    "March": 31,
    "April": 30,
    "May": 31,
    "June": 30,
    "July": 31,
    "August": 31,
```

```python
    "September": 30,
    "October": 31,
    "November": 30,
    "December": 31,
}

# Function to convert month name to number of days
def month_name_to_days(month_name):
    # Convert the month name to title case to handle different capitalization
    month_name = month_name.title()

    # Check if the month name is in the dictionary
    if month_name in month_to_days:
        return month_to_days[month_name]
    else:
        return "Invalid month name"

# Input from the user
month_name = input("Enter a month name: ")

# Call the function and display the result
result = month_name_to_days(month_name)
print(f"The number of days in {month_name} is {result}")
```

DICTIONARIES

1   Prints each item and its corresponding type from the following list.

```python
D = {"hanuman": 10, "3": 'kumar', 44: 'apple', 12.23: 'banana'}
for item in D.items():
    print(type(item[0]))
```

2   To sort (ascending and descending) a dictionary by value

```python
D = {'A': 10, 'a': 12, 'c': 14, 'D': 18}
print(sorted(D.keys()))
print(sorted(D.keys(), reverse=True))
```

3   Add a key to a dictionary

```
D = {'Eid': 523, 'Ename': 'Hanuman', 'Sal': 10000}
D.update({'Add': 'bang'})
print(D)
```

4   Check if a given key already exists in a dictionary.

```
D = {'Eid': 523, 'Ename': 'Hanuman', 'Sal': 10000, 'Add': 'bang'}
key1 = input("Enter key: ")
if key1 in D.keys():
    print(key1, "Exists in dict. ")
else:
    print(key1, "Does not exists.")
```

5   Generate and print a dictionary that contains a number (between 1 and n) in the form (x, x*x)

```
n = int(input("Enter n value:"))
D = {}
for i in range(1, n+1):
    D[i] = i * i
print(D)
```

6   Print a dictionary where the keys are numbers between 1 and 15 (both included) and the values are square of keys

```
D = {}
for i in range(1, 16):
    D[i] = i * i
print(D)
```

7   Merge two Python dictionaries

```
D1 = {'A': 11, 'B': 12, "C": 112}
D2 = {'Z': 20, 'Y': 202, 'X': 100}
D1.update(D2)
print(D1)
```

8   Sum all the items in a dictionary

```
D = {5: 'hello', 2: 'kumar', 10: 234}
print('The sum of keys:', sum(D.keys()))
res = 1
for key in D.keys():
```

```python
  res = res * key
print("Multiplication:", res)
```

9 Multiply all the items in a dictionary

```python
D = {5: 'hello', 2: 'kumar', 10: 234}
print('The sum of keys:', sum(D.keys()))
res = 1
for key in D.keys():
  res = res * key
print("Multiplication:", res)
```

10 Map two lists into a dictionary

```python
Values = [12, 13, 14, 15]
Keys = ['A', 'B', 'C', 'D']
D = dict(zip(Keys, Values))
print(D)
```

11 Sort a dictionary by key

```python
D = {'A': 10, 'B': 23, 'd': 1, 'a': 2}
print(dict(sorted(D.items())))
```

12 Get the maximum and minimum value in a dictionary.

```python
D = {'A': 10, 'Z': 20, 'B': 222, 'X': 2}
print('Max value is:', max(D.values()))
print('Min value is:', min(D.values()))
```

13 Remove duplicates from Dictionary

```python
D = {'A': 10, 'B': 12, 'C': 10, 'D': 11, 'E': 2}
val_list = []
D_new = {}
for key, value in D.items():
  if value not in val_list:
    val_list.append(value)
    D_new[key] = value
print("Given dict:", D)
print("After duplicated removal:", D_new)
```

14 Combine two dictionary adding values for common keys.

```python
dict1 = {'A': 10, 'B': 20, 'E': 25}
dict2 = {'A': 12, 'C': 3}


dict3 = {i: dict1.get(i, 0) + dict2.get(i, 0) for i in set(dict1).union(dict2)}
print(dict3)
```

15   Print all unique values in a dictionary.

```python
dict1 = {'A': 10, 'B': 20, "C": 10, 'D': 12}
for v in dict1.values():
    if list(dict1.values()).count(v) == 1:
        print(v)


print(set(dict1.values()))
```

16   Create and display all combinations of letters, selecting each letter from a different key in a dictionary

```python
import itertools
dict1 = {'A': 1, 'B': 2, 'C': 3, 'D': 4}
L = list(itertools.permutations(dict1.keys()))
print(L)
```

17   Find the highest 3 values in a dictionary.

```python
dict1 = {'A': 11, 'B': 23, 'C': 21, 'D': 34, 'E': 1, 'F': 5}
L = list(dict1.values())
L.sort(reverse=True)
print('The highest three values:', L[0:3])
```

18   Combine values in python list of dictionaries.

```python
L = [{'A': 1, 'B': 2}, {'C': 22, 'D': 12}, {'X': 1, 'Y': 12}]
L1 = []
for subdict in L:
    L1.extend(subdict.values())


print(L1)
```

19   Create a dictionary from a string.

```python
str1 = 'Hello'
dict1 = {}
```

```
for i in str1:
    dict1[i] = str1.count(i)
print(dict1)
```

20   Print a dictionary in table format.

```
dict1 = {'A': 1, 'B': 2, 'C': 3, 'D': 4}
for keys in dict1.keys():
    print(keys, '|', end=' ')
print('\n---------------')
for values in dict1.values():
    print(values, '|', end=' ')
```

21   Count the values associated with key in a dictionary

```
dict1 = {'A': [1, 2, 3], 'B': [2, 3], 'C': 3, 'D': 4}
for keys, values in dict1.items():
    if type(values) == list:
        dict1[keys] = len(values)
    else:
        dict1[keys] = 1
print(dict1)
```

22   Convert a list into a nested dictionary of keys.

```
L = [1, 2, 3, 4]
dict1 = cur = {}

for num in L:
    cur[num] = {}
    cur = cur[num]
print("The nested dict from list:", dict1)
```

23   Sort a list alphabetically in a dictionary.

```
dict1 = {'A': 1, 'a': 3, 'C': 5, 'E': 23}
print(dict1)
dict2 = dict(sorted(dict1.items()))
print(dict2)
```

24   Remove spaces from dictionary keys.

```python
dict1 = {'Hanu ka': 10, 'ha ha': 22, 'HI ku': 50}
dict2 = {}
for key in dict1.keys():
    L = key.split()
    Ls = "".join(L)
    print(Ls)
    dict2[Ls] = dict1[key]
print("The given dict:", dict1)
print("The removed key space dict:", dict2)
```

25   Get the top three items in a shop.

```python
dict1 = {'Apple': 500, 'Banana': 120, 'Cherry': 200, 'Dragon': 320, 'Fruit': 206}
dict2 = {}
# print(dict2)
L = sorted(dict1.values(), reverse=True)
for i in L:
    for k in dict1.keys():
        if dict1[k] == i:
            dict2[k] = dict1[k]
print(dict2)
for ele in list(dict2.keys())[0:3]:
    print(ele)
```

26   To get the key, value and item in a dictionary.

```python
dict1 = {'Apple': 500, 'Banana': 120, 'Cherry': 200, 'Dragon': 320, 'Fruit': 206}
print(dict1.items())
print(dict1.values())
print(dict1.keys())
```

27   print a dictionary line by line.

```python
dict1 = {'Apple': 500, 'Banana': 120, 'Cherry': 200, 'Dragon': 320, 'Fruit': 206}
for item in dict1.items():
    print(item)
```

28   Check multiple keys exists in a dictionary.

```
dict1 = {'Apple': 500, 'Banana': 120, 'Cherry': 200, 'Dragon': 320, 'Fruit': 206}
# dict2 = {'A': 10}
if len(list(dict1.keys())) > 1:
   print("Multiple keys exists:")
else:
   print("No multiple keys.")
```

29   Count number of items in a dictionary value that is a list

```
dict1 = {'Apple': [500, 10, 20], 'Banana': [120, 10],  'Cherry': 200, 'Dragon': 320, 'Fruit': [20, 1]}
count = 0
for key, value in dict1.items():
   if type(value) == list:
      count += 1
if count > 0:
   print("The no of keys with list value:", count)
else:
   print("No keys with list values.")
```

30   Sort Counter by value.

```
dict1 = {'Apple': 500, 'Banana': 120, 'Cherry': 200, 'Dragon': 320, 'Fruit': 206}
dict2 = {}
# print(dict2)
L = sorted(dict1.values(), reverse=True)
for i in L:
   for k in dict1.keys():
      if dict1[k] == i:
         dict2[k] = dict1[k]
print(dict2)
```

31   create a dictionary from two lists without losing duplicate values.

```
L1 = [1, 2, 3, 4]
L2 = [10, 2, 3, 15]
dict1 = {K: V for K, V in zip(L1, L2)}
print(dict1)
```

32   Replace dictionary values with their sum.

```
dict1 = {'Apple': [500, 10, 20], 'Banana': [120, 10],  'Cherry': 200, 'Dragon': 320, 'Fruit': [20, 1]}
dict2 = {}
for key, value in dict1.items():
   if type(value) == list:
      dict2[key] = sum(value)
   else:
      dict2[key] = value
print(dict2)
```

33   Match key values in two dictionaries.

```
dict1 = {'Apple': [500, 10, 20], 'Banana': [120, 10],  'Cherry': 200, 'Dragon': 320, 'Fruit': [20, 1]}
dict2 = {'Banana': [120, 10],  'Cherry': 200, 'Dragon': 320, 'DDD': 100}

L = [item for item in dict1.items() if item in dict2.items()]
print(L)
```


TUPLE

1   create a tuple.

```
T = (1, 2, 3, 4, 10)
print(type(T))
T1 = (1, 'Hanuman', 12.65, True)
print(type(T1))
print("The type of tuple elements:", T1)
for ele in T1:
   print(type(ele), end='')
```

2   create a tuple with different data types

```
T = (1, 2, 3, 4, 10)
print(type(T))
T1 = (1, 'Hanuman', 12.65, True)
print(type(T1))
print("The type of tuple elements:", T1)
for ele in T1:
   print(type(ele), end='')
```

3   create a tuple with numbers and print one item

```python
T = (1, 3, 4, 6)
print("The element at 2nd index:", T[2])
```

4   unpack a tuple in several variables

```python
T = (11, 22, 34)
(a, b, c) = T
(x, *y) = T
print("Unpacking with all variables:", a, b, c)
print("Unpacking with arbitrary variable:", x, y)
print(y)
print(y[0])
```

5   add an item in a tuple.

```python
T = (22, 23, 34, 45)
x = (100,)
T = T + x
print(T)
```

6   convert a tuple to a string

```python
T = (1, 22, 34, 45)
new_str = ''
for ele in T:
    new_str = new_str + str(ele)
print(new_str)
```

7   get the 4th element and 4th element from last of a tuple

```python
T = (1, 3, 44, 55, 6, 2, 29, 23, 61, 76)
print("The first 4th element:", T[3])
print("THe last 4th element:", T[-4])
```

8   create the colon of a tuple

```python
T = (34, 45, [], 23)
print("The given tuple is:", T)
T[2].append(1000)
print("The new tuple:", T)
```

9   find the repeated items of a tuple

```
T = (11, 22, 33, 45, 22, 11, 34)
L = []
for ele in T:
   if T.count(ele) > 1:
      L.append(ele)
print(tuple(set(L)))
```

10   check whether an element exists within a tuple

```
T = (11, 22, 33, 45, 22, 11, 34)
ele = int(input("Enter element to chk:"))
for e in T:
   if ele == e:
      print("Element Found.")
      break
else:
   print("Element Not Found.")
```

11   convert a list to a tuple

```
L = [1, 2, 3, 4, 5]
T = tuple(L)
print(type(L), type(T))
```

12   remove an item from a tuple

```
T = (12, 23, 44, 55)
LT = list(T)
ele = int(input("Enter element to delete:"))
if ele in LT:
   LT. remove(ele)
   print(tuple(LT))
else:
   print("Element not Present")
```

13   slice a tuple

```
T = (1, 2, 3, 4, 5, 67, 56, 22)
print("The first three elements:", T[0:3])
print("The even position elements:", T[::2])
print(T[::-1])
```

14   find the index of an item of a tuple.

```
T = (1, 2, 3, 4, 5, 67, 56, 22)
print("the index of last element", T.index(T[-1]))
```

15   find the length of a tuple

```
T = (1, 2, 3, 4, 5, 67, 56, 22)
print("The length of tuple:", len(T))
```

16   convert a tuple to a dictionary

```
T = ((1, 2), (2, 11), (3, 1))
D = dict(T)

print("the dict from tuple:", D)
```

17   unzip a list of tuples into individual lists.

```
L = [(1, 22), (2, 33), (3, 44)]
D = dict(L)
L1 = list(D.keys())
L2 = list(D.values())
print("Unzip list of tuples:", L1, L2)
```

18   reverse a tuple.

```
T = (11, 22, 33, 4, 5, 6)
print("The given tuple:", T)
print("The reversed tuple:", T[::-1])
```

19   convert a list of tuples into a dictionary

```
L = [(1, 22), (2, 33), (3, 44)]
D = dict(L)
print(D)
```

20   print a tuple with string formatting

```
T = (1, 2, 3, 4, 5, 67, 56, 22)
print("The string formatting {} tuple".format(T))
```

21   replace last value of tuples in a list

```
T = (1, 2, 3, 4, 5, 67, 56, 22)
LT = list(T)
print("The given tuple is:", T)
LT[-1] = 100
print("The replace tuple:", tuple(LT))
```

22   to remove an empty tuple(s) from a list of tuples

```
L = [(1, 2), (), (2, 3), (22, 33)]
print("The given list of tuples:", L)
for t in L:
    if len(t) == 0:
        L.remove(t)
print("The updated list of tuples:", L)
```

23   sort a tuple by its float element.

```
T = (12.2, 11.3, 44.5, 12, 23)
print(sorted(T))
```

24   count the elements in a list until an element is a tuple

```
L = [10.3, 11, 'hanuman', (4,), (2, 3, 4), 16]
C = 0
for ele in L:
    if type(ele) == tuple:
        break
    else:
        C += 1

print("The non list count till list type:", C)
```

SET

1   Create a set. 2 Iteration over sets. 3   Add member(s) in a set.

4   Remove item(s) from set , 5   Remove an item from a set if it is present in the set.

```
S = {11, 22, 33, 44, 55, 12, 14}
print("The given set:", S)
print("The elements in set are..")
for ele in S:
```

```python
    print(ele, end=' ')
S.add(100)
print("After addition of 100:", S)
S.remove(55)
print("After removal of 55:", S)
```

6   Create an intersection of sets, 7   Create a union of sets, 8   Create set difference

9   Create a symmetric difference.

```python
S1 = {10, 11, 23, 44, 1}
S2 = {10, 23, 1, 3}
print("Union:", S1.union(S2))
print("Intersection:", S1.intersection(S2))
print('SetDifference', S1.difference(S2))
print('Symdifference', S1.symmetric_difference(S2))
```

10   Issubset and issuperset.

```python
S1 = {10, 11, 23, 44}
S2 = {10, 23, 44}
print('S2 is subset of S1:', S2.issubset(S1))
print('S1 is superset of S2', S1.issuperset(S2))
```

11   Create a shallow copy of sets.,   12 Clear a set.

```python
S1 = {10, 11, 23, 44}
S2 = S1
S3 = S1.copy()
S2.add(100)
S3.add(300)
print("Shallow copy(added 100)", 'S1-', S1, 'S2-', S2)
print("Deep copy(added 300)--the S3 and S1", S3, S1)
```

13   Use of frozen sets

```python
S = {12, 22, 34, 1}
S = frozenset(S)
print(S)
```

14   Find maximum and the minimum value in a set, 15 Find the length of a set

```
S = {12, 22, 34, 1, 10, 15, 19}
print("The max is {} and min is {} in set. ".format(max(S), min(S)))
print("The length of set is:", len(S))
```

ARRAYS

1   Create an array of 5 integers and display the array items. Access individual element through indexes.

```
import array
A = array.array('i', [12, 13, 14, 10, 20])


for i in A:
   print(i)
```

2   Append a new item to the end of the array., 3 Reverse the order of the items in the array.

```
import array
A = array.array('i', [12, 13, 14, 10, 20])
A.append(500)
print("The array elements:", A[:])
print("The reverse:", A[::-1])
```

4   Get the length in bytes of one array item in the internal representation, 5 Get the current memory address and the length in elements of the buffer used to hold an arrays? contents and also find the size

```
import array
A = array.array('i', [12, 13, 14, 10, 20])
print("the size of element in array:", A.itemsize)
print("The memory address of array is:", id(A))
print("The buffer information:", A.buffer_info())
```

6   Get the number of occurrences of a specified element in an array

```
import array
A = array.array('i', [12, 13, 14, 10, 20, 10, 10])
ele = int(input("Enter element to find count:"))
print("The element count is:", A.count(ele))
```

7   Append items from inerrable to the end of the array

```
import array
A = array.array('i', [12, 13, 14, 10, 20, 10, 10])
print("Before Append:", A)
A.append(500)
print("After append:", A)
```

8   Convert an array to an array of machine values and return the bytes representation

```
import array
A = array.array('b', [12, 13, 14, 10, 20, 10, 10])
print(A.tobytes())
```

9   Append items from a specified list.

```
import array
A = array.array('i', [12, 13, 14, 10, 20, 10, 10])
L = [1, 2, 3]
for i in L:
    A.append(i)
print("After list append:", A)
```

10   Insert a new item before the second element in an existing array.

```
import array
A = array.array('i', [12, 13, 14, 10, 20, 10, 10])
A.insert(1, 300)
print("after insertion of element 300 at 2nd before:", A)
```

11   Remove a specified item using the index from an array.

```
import array
A = array.array('i', [12, 13, 14, 10, 20, 10, 10])
print("4th index item removed", A.pop(4))
```

12   Remove the first occurrence of a specified element from an array.

```
import array
A = array.array('i', [12, 13, 14, 10, 20, 10, 10])
A.remove(10)
print("First occurrence of item removed", A)
```

13   Convert an array to an ordinary list with the same items.

```
import array
A = array.array('i', [12, 13, 14, 10, 20, 10, 10])
L = list(A)
print("The given array is:", A)
print("The converted list:", L)
```